Alan Kreider

p 43
p 53 — The Resolve p. 93
p 64 Sources

COMMUNITY OF THE TRANSFIGURATION

NML NEW MONASTIC LIBRARY
Resources for Radical Discipleship

For over a millennium, if Christians wanted to read theology, practice Christian spirituality, or study the Bible, they went to the monastery to do so. There, people who inhabited the tradition and prayed the prayers of the church also copied manuscripts and offered fresh reflections about living the gospel in a new era. Two thousand years after the birth of the church, a new monastic movement is stirring in North America. In keeping with ancient tradition, new monastics study the classics of Christian reflection and are beginning to offer some reflections for a new era. The New Monastic Library includes reflections from new monastics as well as classic monastic resources unavailable elsewhere.

Series Editor: Jonathan Wilson-Hartgrove

VOL. 1: *School(s) for Conversion*, edited by members
of the Rutba House

VOL. 2: *Inhabiting the Church*, by Jon Stock, Tim Otto,
and Jonathan Wilson-Hartgrove

Community of the
TRANSFIGURATION

The
Journey
of a
New
Monastic
Community

PAUL R. DEKAR
with a foreword by PHYLLIS TICKLE

CASCADE *Books* • Eugene, Oregon

COMMUNITY OF THE TRANSFIGURATION
The Journey of a New Monastic Community

New Monastic Library: Resources for Radical Discipleship 3

Cascade Books
A Division of Wipf and Stock Publishers
199 W. 8th Ave., Suite 3
Eugene, OR 97401

www.wipfandstock.com

ISBN 13: 978-1-55635-430-4

Cataloging-in-Publication data:

Dekar, Paul R.
    Community of the Transfiguration : the journey of a new monastic community /
    Paul R. Dekar.

    New Monastic Library: Resources for Radical Discipleship 3

    xxiv + 162 p.; 23 cm.

    ISBN 13: 978-1-55635-430-4

    1. Community of the Transfiguration (Australia)—history. 2. Monasticism
and religious orders—rules. 3. Communities—Religious aspects—Christianity.
4. Christian life. I. Title. II. Series.

BV4407.2 .D34 2008

Manufactured in the U.S.A.

To my sisters and brothers of the Community of the Transfiguration, beloved of the Holy One Who lightens our paths. May God continue to bless you as you journey in compassion, creativity, integrity, and radical love.

CONTENTS

Phyllis Tickle

On January 14, 1935, Dietrich Bonhoeffer wrote a portentous letter to his brother, Karl-Friedrick. What Bonhoeffer, now famously, said in that letter was to prove both prophetic and affirming to that which it predicted. He wrote, "the restoration of the church will surely come only from a new type of monasticism which has nothing in common with the old but a complete lack of compromise in a life lived in accordance with the Sermon on the Mount in the discipleship of Christ. I think it is time to gather people together to do this."

One can argue that the exquisite horror of burgeoning Nazism lent a singular clarity to Bonhoeffer's perceptions and, therefore, to the providential accuracy of his assessment. This does not account for the fact, however, that within thirty years of his letter to Karl-Friedrick, and within twenty-five years of his own martyrdom at the hands of the Nazis, a new monasticism was aborning all over western Christendom. Most frequently referred to now as "the new monasticism" or "neomonasticism," the vocation to intentional, communal life in radical pursuit of the way of Jesus of Nazareth had spread, by 1970, across two oceans and across dozens of geopolitical borders. Christians were hearing, for the first time in many centuries, the intonations of that for which Bonhoeffer's letter had been only the introit.

For over a millennium and a half, when a Christian said the word *monasticism*, it was understood that he or she was referring to a celibate, often sequestered form of communal life functioning under the imprimatur or privilege of Roman, Orthodox, or Anglican episcopacy. This mold, as Bonhoeffer had hoped, has been forever broken in our time. No longer limited to the unencumbered, almost all of the new intentional communities have both married and/or familied members as well as celibate ones; the vows of all are identical, save that the single who wishes to may take the added vow of celibacy. Likewise, today's neo-monastic communities almost eschew sequestration. They see their call to be defined, in part, by the larger community in which they live. Their rejoicing before God and their thanksgiving before Christ are best realized for them in love-motivated service to immediate and present neighbors, especially to the destitute and rejected in whose urban despair many of the new monastics choose to live and be.

Most startling of all, of course, is the fact that the neo-monastic communities, by and large, are more often Protestant in heritage than Roman or Orthodox. As such, they often operate out of the principle of accountability to one another and their Lord, rather than to some overarching, ecclesial structure. And most tellingly, because most of them have come up out of Protestant formation, these new monastics are unencumbered by the hundreds of layers of rubrics, edicts, and traditions that have managed, over the centuries, to bury (not to mention embalm) much of historic Christian liturgy and discipline. Free of natal prejudices, they come rejoicing to the sacred meal as the central expression of oneness and to the keeping of sacred time as a blessed pacing for the soul's exercise. They fast, pray the offices, feed the poor, and tend those sick in spirit, mind, or body. They also do what every vowed community should do: They actively confess themselves to one another and work together for the perfection of call in each other.

Even when all this has been said, however, the pages that follow here may still come initially as a shock for some readers. The pages that follow here are the history—the story, really—of Holy Transfiguration Monastery (HTM), which is located in Breakwater, Australia. The surprise is that HTM is Baptist in origin and in province, the community being an active, subordinate, and tithing part of the Baptist Union of Victoria. Although there is no requirement at HTM that a postulant be Baptist either in heritage or present practice, or that there be re-baptism by immersion as a condition of acceptance, there is still a clear recognition of Baptist origin and Baptist polity. This last set of circumstances is, moreover, part of the fascination that Paul Dekar's history of HTM holds for me personally.

There are undoubtedly hundreds of neo-monastic communities in the United States alone. Indeed, so far as I know, there is nothing close to a master list from which to begin to estimate their numbers. Some are near enough to one another geographically to achieve a kind of critical mass in public awareness. Church of the Apostles (COTA), Mustard Seed House, and Monkfish Abbey are all in Seattle, for instance; and The Simple Way and New Jerusalem are both in Philadelphia. Some, like Rutba House in Durham, are so often referenced by other, newer communities as to have achieved a form of general visibility. And some, like the Community of Jesus in Orleans, Massachusetts, have become so large and so actively present as Christ's laborers in the world at large as to be visible almost by default.

The Community of Jesus is my Holy Transfiguration Monastery. That is, like HTM, it has a strong heritage of Baptist, as well as Presbyterian and Episcopalian, roots; is richly observant of the traditional praxis of the Church; evangelizes by and through the arts; and succors those who come to it, even as it reaches out to those who need but cannot come.

When, in other words, Paul Dekar talks about his decade-plus of interest in and involvement with his fellow-Christians in HTM, I have to admit that were he to change the initials "HTM" to "C of J" and the locale from Breakwater, Australia, to Orleans, MA, he would be speaking my truth. Originally, in fact, it was my own decade-plus of involvement from afar with, and ever-increasing ties of godly affection for, the C of J that caused me to become interested in Dekar's work. Now, sometime later and with his history completed, it is Dekar's gifts that are equally compelling for me.

What Dekar has managed to do here is tell his own story, a monastery's story, and a movement's story in such a way as to make them all of one piece. Like layers of a well-rendered landscape, each gives depth and texture to the other, each lends grace to the other. Because Dekar is an academic by trade, there is here the academic's care for analysis and contextualization. Because he is an observant Christian, there is nuance and insight that a secular historian could never bring to the work. Because he is a storyteller at heart, there is a charm and delight here that neither the careful academic nor the devout believer alone could produce.

Finally, of course, as with any good story, be it history, account, or something of both, there is news here. In this case, the news is of other Christians and their ways of devotion, of other winds of the Spirit blowing across our times, and of other witnesses for whose encouragement we can pray. May each of us find in all these things reason to rejoice, as well as a passion and devotion by which to measure and amend our own.

Phyllis Tickle
Fifteenth Week of Ordinary Time, 2007

The renewal of Christian monasticism is the great spiritual movement of our day. Imbued with a love for God and neighbor, and with a healthy self-love, people are going to monasteries to deepen their relationship with God, to pray, and to find peace. While some religious institutions are suffering a decline in traditional vocations, others are experiencing renewal. Christians are exploring new monastic lifestyles. Congregations are birthing new monasteries and monastic-like intentional communities. Like the wind from God that swept over the waters at the time of creation (Gen 1:2), the Holy Spirit is moving among individuals and institutions. We are riding the crest of a tsunami that has not yet broken.

Monastic vocations are open to an exciting future. Shane Claiborne, one of the founding members of The Simple Way in Philadelphia, Pennsylvania, characterizes the phenomenon called the new monasticism as a revolution that begins inside little people, guerrilla peacemakers, and dancing prophets. Claiborne writes that these revolutionaries love, laugh, and, through acts of love, are making a huge difference in local communities throughout the western world. He invites ordinary people everywhere to "begin to be Christians again." Prayerfully, he concludes, "Jesus, give us the courage."[1]

In 1998, my wife Nancy and I journeyed to Melbourne in the State of Victoria, Australia. We resided at Whitley College of the Melbourne College of Divinity, where Athol Gill had taught from 1975 until his sudden death in 1992. Gill's writing and leadership in the House of the Gentle Bunyip, an ecumenical Christian community, had inspired

1. Claiborne, *Irresistible Revolution*, 356.

my initial desire to spend time in Australia. I was teaching a course on holistic witness, an introduction to the mission of the church, when I learned that the Bunyip was about to close. I discovered other intentional communities scattered in or near Melbourne. One, the Community of the Transfiguration, was located in Breakwater, a suburb of Geelong, fifty miles southwest of Melbourne.

Whitley colleague Merrill Kitchen invited us to accompany her to attend a liturgy at the Breakwater Community, as it is commonly called, or Holy Transfiguration Monastery (HTM). We went one Thursday. The beauty of the grounds, the welcome of Community members, and the powerful worship impressed us. We were at Breakwater but a few hours and regretted the brevity of this visit. At the time, we were unaware that God had opened up a new path on our journeys of faith, a road that still leads into the future.

In late 1999, I prepared to return to Melbourne for the Fourth International Baptist Peace Conference on "Hearing the Cry, Acting in Hope" and for meetings of the Baptist World Alliance. I was to continue on to an Aboriginal settlement and to India for other commitments. Nancy could not accompany me.

I shared plans with a friend who had lived in Australia for many years. The failure of her relationship with her partner had led to her separation from a teenager she had co-parented. This disruption contributed to problems the young person was experiencing. My friend had had no recent communication with her former partner, but she did know that her son and his birthmother lived in Geelong with a connection to some sort of community. She feared that, in his vulnerable state, her son had been sucked into an obscure cult. In those pre-Google days, she did not know that it was an innovative Baptist monastery.

I discovered that the Community was providing the young person counseling as well as other forms of support for him and his birthmother. With wide consultation, I facilitated a renewed relationship between my friend and her son.

The ability of this group to offer all the parties involved a genuinely real and radical love was truly extraordinary. I was impressed to see how members live with a remarkable degree of integrity, imagination, and Christ-likeness. I found myself being drawn to the Community and to the journey of members in Christian discipleship.

The Community invited me to spend a few days at the Cloister on retreat, and I spoke about one of the key monastic influences on the Community, Thomas Merton (1915–1968). Again in 2002, when I was able to return to Australia for a couple months, I sought out the Community. A way opened for me to spend three days on retreat at Breakwater. During my visit, members invited me to return with Nancy, conduct research, and write about the Community.

As part of the process of discernment, I questioned Community members whether they had considered possible implications of any publication or public presentation. For example, articles, a book, a video, or a keyword entered into an Internet search might elicit a deluge of requests for information or visits that the Community could not accommodate. Due to time constraints, limited resources, and other priorities, the Community cannot offer hospitality to large numbers of guests who might want to spend time in the Community. True to monastic tradition, the Community was already receiving an amazing number of visitors.

This was not the first time that the Community had considered sharing its life more widely. After a couple of false starts, it had chosen not to do so in part due to its desire to protect the privacy of persons, especially children and former members. Over the past thirty-five years, five persons have left the Community, and none of these departures were cordial or smooth. Community members expressed some concern about exposing these struggles in public.

Understanding that there is always grief and responsibility for the breakdown in relationships on both sides, I alerted Community members of my sensitivity to their concerns. They assured me they would be open, transparent, and vulnerable about their personal and collective journeys. I agreed to explore with Nancy if and when I might undertake this project. Without promise or expectation as to what would follow, Nancy and I spent two months at Breakwater in 2004, a month in 2005, and a month in 2006. I returned for a month in 2007.

We shared fully in the Community's rhythm of prayer, work, and study. Moved by the liturgies and daily offices, we often found ourselves down on our knees in grateful praise. Other aspects of the life of the Community were equally compelling: the power of the personal stories of members and Companions; the support the sisters and brothers offer one another in every aspect of living; the love of the brothers and sisters for the natural world, for youth, and for marginalized persons; the care by which the grounds are maintained; and the rich use of the visual arts. At times we felt embarrassed by the generosity of the Community. For both of us, forty years of membership in Baptist congregations had not prepared us for this new thing, a Baptist monastery.

During these sojourns I conducted over a hundred interviews with members, companions, and friends. Through their life in the Community of the Transfiguration, many have found healing of deep wounds. In turn, some have claimed a role as a "wounded healer," a phrase I owe to spiritual writer Henri J. M. Nouwen (1932–1996).

HTM members and Companions have accompanied many people, especially the dechurched, on a journey from painful experiences in their Christian past to healing, from superficiality to their truest self, from darkness to light, and from fragmentation to wholeness. The radical love Community members have extended to lay people, pastors, denominational leaders, critics, and even enemies is perhaps its greatest gift. Many outside the Community confirm this judgment. For example, Dr. Tom Paterson, a registered psychologist with the Relationship Centre in Melbourne and a therapist for many Community members, describes the Community as an inspiring source of hope for the world. For Paterson, HTM offers not a panacea, but a pathway for those who can accept its challenges.[2]

In the First Testament,[3] we read that Abraham interceded before God on behalf of Sodom and Gomorrah, "What if ten righteous are there?" God answered, "For the sake of ten I will not destroy it" (Gen 18:32). According to the legend of the *Lamed Vov*, transmitted through Hasidic tradition and absorbed by me from my Jewish roots, the story goes on to affirm that on earth at any time are Thirty-six Just. Unaware that their prayer and service are as pillars holding up the earth, these upright individuals allay the wrath of God and prevent earth's destruction.[4]   Russian author Alexander Solzhenitsyn draws on this tradition in his story of Matryona, a proverbial grandmother, *babushka*.

2. Paterson, "Family Therapy and the Good Life," 8.

3. To identify Hebrew Scripture shared by Christians and Jews I use "First Testament" rather than "Old Testament." "Second Testament" refers to the "New Testament." In relationships among Jews and Christians, the words old and new can have negative connotations.

4. Scholem, *Messianic Idea in Judaism,* 251–56; Wiesel, *Legends of Our Time,* 125–29.

Misunderstood and rejected by her husband, a stranger to her
own family despite her happy, amiable temperament, comical,
so foolish that she worked for others for no reward, this woman,
who had buried all her six children, had stored up no earthly
goods. Nothing but a dirty white goat, a lame cat, and a row of
fig plants.

None of us who lived close to her perceived that she was that
one righteous person without whom, as the saying goes, no city
can stand.

Neither can the whole world.[5]

Mindful that we all bear the divine image and likeness, I believe anyone
can be one of the righteous ones who are equal in dignity to Abraham
and Sarah, Isaac and Rebecca, Jacob and Rachel. Yet, surely at Breakwater
I have met some of the Thirty-Six Just. Through their prayers and service,
Community members offer a holistic witness to God in contemporary
society. Friends and members have centered their lives in Christ not as
a doctrine, but as a person. They offer themselves as hands and feet by
which the hospitality of God, the compassion of Jesus, and the dynamism
of the Holy Spirit are manifest in the world.

Many titles dealing with monasticism and intentional communities
already exist. One may ask whether there is a need for a book about this
tiny seed of God's realm. For at least three reasons, my response is af-
firmative. First, in North America and around the world, both inside and
outside the church, there are many who have lost a faith that they once
valued or have left a body of believers deeply wounded or have never
been part of any faith community. Without disparaging the validity of
other expressions of Christian institutional life, HTM members seek to
manifest the message of the Gospel in a way that promotes relationship
with God first, then the creation of time and space for spiritual growth
and personal liberation. With other new monastic communities, the
Community of the Transfiguration offers a compelling vision of the in-
breaking realm of God, an ancient yet fresh spirituality, and an invitation
to all persons to experience of the Creator of life.

Second, the manifestations of Christianity one experiences or hears
about are all too often negative. People need exemplars of a different and
more positive expression of faith, one that stands out as a clear sign of the

5. Solzhenitsyn, *Stories and Prose Poems*, 41–42.

reign of God.[6] If readers gain a sense of meaning, direction, and support from reading this book, it will have realized two significant goals: to document how members of a local congregation and intentional community have been transfigured and enabled to transform their neighborhood in constructive ways; and to extrapolate from this case study principles and ideas that may inform the interest in community of others who are not necessarily called to such an expression of Christian monasticism.

Finally, we live in dangerous times. Amidst dark days of dashed hopes, in which people are prepared to take necessary, costly steps to end war, make affluence history, or mitigate adverse environmental consequences of global warming, HTM members offer a vocation of radical resistance to the secular, individualistic, and consumerist culture of which they are a part. After a generation of living according to the values and practices of "the dream of God," a phrase of Verna J. Dozier (1917–2006), Community members have shared the journey to which they believe they have been called. When asked if hope or authentic communities are possible in postmodern society, I point to the Community and the calling of its members to do justice, love with compassion, and walk humbly with God (Mic 6:8).

Of all themes that emerge from this study, the one that stands out for me is the radical nature of Christian community. According to the *Oxford English Dictionary*, the word *radical* comes from the Latin *radix* for roots. The basic idea has to do with acting upon or touching what is basic or essential. As used in this book, the phrase *radical witness* or *radical love* suggests something inherent in Christian discipleship. In Antioch, early followers of the risen Christ lived in such a way that it was there that the disciples were first called "Christians" (Acts 11:26). In another usage of the word, rare in the earliest canonical writings, Christians glorified God by obeying the gospel (1 Pet 4:16). In Pauline thought, Christians were rooted and grounded in love (Eph 3:17). Elsewhere, Paul encouraged his faithful brothers and sisters in Christ in Colossae to continue to live their lives in Christ. Rooted and built up in Christ and established in the faith, they lived as they were taught and abounded in thanksgiving (Col 2:6–7).

The Community of the Transfiguration recalls for me the radical witness of early Christians and also an image in the novel, *The Last*

6. Langmead, *Reimagining God and Mission*, xxiii.

Western by Thomas S. Klise. The book tells the story of Willie, an Irish-Indian-Negro-Chinese boy who grows up in abject poverty but whose baseball skills are manifest in the slums and sandlots of Houston. Willie can pitch. Typical of so many of our athlete heroes, he makes a quick ascent to major league baseball. In his first game, he strikes out twenty-seven consecutive players. He becomes a national sensation, but quickly finds that the baseball executives are exploiting him.

When race riots strike his home area, Willie leaves his team and returns to Houston where his family and friends are dead and his home razed. Overcome by horror, he runs, eventually collapsing. Some people who call themselves the Silent Servants of the Used, Abused, and Utterly Screwed Up find him and nurse him back to health. Here is Thomas Klise's description of this radical community:

> The Servants will always choose the way of serving the poor, the lonely, the despised, the outcast, the miserable and the misfit. The mission of the Servants is to prove to the unloved that they are not abandoned, nor finally left alone. Hence, the natural home of the Servants is strife, misfortune, crisis, the falling apart of things. The Society cherishes failure for it is in failure, in trouble, in the general breaking up of classes, stations, usual conditions, normal routines that human hearts are open to the light of God's mercy.[7]

Willie subsequently joins the Silent Servants of the Used, Abused, and Utterly Screwed Up. Though very few of us are fully able to identify with Willie, there is a sense in which we are all Willies. We need to become part of healing communities. In our hedonistic, individualistic, and materialistic society, it is amongst trusted friends that we may experience forgiveness and healing on a journey that leads to freedom.

Writing is by nature intensely personal and ultimately autobiographical. Stephen Muecke, who teaches cultural studies at the University of Technology in Sydney, Australia, characterizes it as tracing a path that readers can follow into the space of the next creation.[8] I trust that the traces I present here, reflections on my own life journey and on the experience of HTM members and Companions, will help readers to find encouragement for the long journey ahead to human interdependence one with another, with creation, and with the God whom we adore.

7. Klise, *Last Western*, 150.
8. Muecke, *No Road (Bitumen All the Way)*, 231.

OUTLINE

Having introduced very briefly how I came to be involved with the Community of the Transfiguration, I now turn to describing its life within the wider framework of monastic renewal. Among themes we will explore are principles that emerge from this study that are relevant to church and society at large.

Chapter 1 briefly summarizes the history of renewal movements within western monasticism through the latter decades of the twentieth century with the Catholic reforms of Vatican II and the emergence of new monastic movements. Chapter 2 has a brief summary of HTM's history, with a longer account for those interested. Chapter 3 describes the practices of Community members. Chapter 4 explores the theology of the Resolve. In Chapter 5, we assess HTM's monastic engagement in its context and gifts that are potentially life-giving for anyone, not just for readers called to the monastic life or even to Christian faith. An Appendix supplements prayers and liturgies scattered through the text, followed by a bibliography.

Convinced that the Earth is at great risk, I believe this story of HTM and the radical witness of the new monastics have implications for what is meant by the Hebrew expression *tikkun olam*—the repair of God's creation and of faith. Describing this idea, the seventeenth-century Jewish mystic Isaac Luria said that the Creator of the Universe, deciding to make a world, drew in the divine breath—contracted—in order to make room for the creation coming into being. In this enlarged space, the Creator then set vessels and poured into the vessels the radiance of the divine light. But the light was too brilliant for the vessels, which shattered and scattered all over the place. Since that time, the work of humans has been to pick up and to try to mend or refashion the shards of creation.

Contemporary scholars Emil Fackenheim, Maria Harris, Michael Lerner, and others have developed this concept in the aftermath of the *Shoah* (holocaust). In light of failure of moral action during this twentieth-century catastrophe, can twenty-first-century monastic spirituality prod us to a *tikkun*-sense of things: care, awe, appreciation of sacredness, and love?[9]

Throughout the text, I address possible concerns of some readers, especially those who are spiritual heirs of the sixteenth-century Protestant

---

9. Harris, *Proclaim Jubilee!*, 15.

revolution. Their forebears rejected monasticism for several reasons. One was Biblical: nowhere did they read of a requirement that Christians should take vows such as obedience to a person or perpetual celibacy. Another was theological: they regarded monastic spirituality as a type of works-righteousness that contradicted the message of free grace. Finally, monasticism seemed to violate the priesthood of all believers by creating an elite at the apex of a spiritual hierarchy.

LANGUAGE

In matters of contemporary English usage, the topic of this book poses particular challenges. Often, the word monk, derived from the Greek *monos*, meaning alone or solitary, refers to men only. The word nun refers to female monastics.

The Orthodox Christian tradition makes no distinction between a monastery for men and a monastery for women. The Catholic tradition distinguishes between the monasteries of male monks and convents of female nuns. Both groups take vows of stability, obedience, and conversion of life, which includes the ideas of poverty and chastity. As well, there are the third orders that the church recognizes as equal in every respect though called to live family life outside the monastery. And there are the "religious," including priests like the Jesuits or sisters like the Missionaries of Charity, the order of Mother Teresa of Calcutta (1910–1997).

Some Protestant traditions, notably churches coming out of the sixteenth-century Anabaptist and eighteenth-century Pietist movements, have placed great emphasis on the common life and have spawned many intentional communities. Other traditions that arose during the sixteenth-century Reformation, notably the Anglican and Lutheran churches, have continued to have small monastic communities of men, women, or men and women.

In this book, the word *monastery* refers to communities of men, of women, or of men and women. In some new monastic communities, couples live in the community with their children. The word *monk* refers to male and female monastics. Among the special vows by which a monk commits herself or himself to a particular monastery is chastity, which is understood as sexual purity and, possibly but not necessarily, celibacy.

Monasteries provide for dispersed members called lay associates, companions or, in the case of Benedictines, *oblates*. Unlike Medieval

Europe, when *oblates* took vows and wore habits unique to particular monasteries, now lay monastics are life-professed and share to the best of their ability in the rhythm of prayer, study, and work of a specific community. They have responded to awareness that God has called them to serve God and neighbor.

Members of some monastic communities do not use their surnames and in some instances receive a new name. I refer to HTM members as brother or sister and their given name. I provide full names in footnotes only. When quoting authors who use male language to express inclusive ideas, I do not change the text. Otherwise, I try to write inclusively throughout the book. Unless indicated otherwise, all references to Scripture are from the New Revised Standard Version.

The Community of the Transfiguration refers to a dispersed community for which several names have been used. HTM refers mainly to the Cloister located at Breakwater until early 2008 when Community members begin to move to their new property at Teesdale. Around Victoria, people speak of the Community of the Transfiguration. I use HTM and Community of the Transfiguration interchangeably.

WORDS OF APPRECIATION

This book has arisen from commitments I have made as a Christian, as a husband, father, and grandfather, and as a scholar. Many people have helped me along the way, especially Nancy. My wife for forty years, Nancy lives our prayers and prays our lives. She has participated fully in our journey with the Community of the Transfiguration.

This book is very much the outcome of a collegial process. Taking a great risk in sharing the most intimate aspects of their spiritual journeys with me, and now with readers, members of the Community of the Transfiguration have responded generously to requests for interviews, documents, and information. Cloister, Skete, and Greater Community members have read the entire manuscript in draft. Mike Dugdale, companion of the Community, took the photographs.

I am indebted to the Lilly Foundation for a Research Expense Grant that permitted me to travel to Australia in 2004, and again in 2005. Memphis Theological Seminary, where I have been a member of faculty since January 1995, granted me a research leave during the spring term of 2007 to write this book. I am indebted to colleagues who carried a greater workload and to a library staff that was ever ready to assist me. Particularly helpful in tracking down obscure sources without which I could not have completed this book were Jane Williamson, Assistant Director responsible for inter-library loans; Susan Stewart, Catalogue Librarian; Mildred Saulsberry, Circulation Librarian; and Melissa Hamblin, who procures new materials.

Rob Baker, Billy Bickers, Jack Conrad, Nancy Rose Dekar, Jeff Gros, John Kilzer, Ross Lawford, Marguerite Dekar Li, Stacy Li, William Northrup, Wendy Scott, and Billy Vaughan read and made suggestions about drafts, as did Community members. I am accountable for suggestions not incorporated into the final text.

Two individuals warrant special recognition. Memphian Phyllis A. Tickle is a publisher, speaker, contributing editor in religion for *Publishers Weekly*, and author or editor of over twenty books. In 1996, Phyllis received the 1996 Mays Award, one of the book industry's most prestigious awards for lifetime achievement in writing and publishing, and specifically in recognition of her work in gaining mainstream media coverage of religious publishing. She expresses her enthusiasm for this project in her Foreword.

As editor, Jonathan Wilson-Hartgrove of Rutba House, a new monastic community in Durham, North Carolina, has given the manuscript careful attention at every step of the way. Due to unanticipated circumstances, I could not visit Rutba House as planned in late 2006. I hope to correct this in the near future. I am grateful to Jonathan for his support for this project.

I am grateful to editors for use of material published in newsletters of the Oblates of St. John's Abbey, a monastery of Benedictine Catholic men in Collegeville, Minnesota, and the Baptist Peace Fellowship of North America. Scholarly articles that have appeared include, "Monastic Renewal in Australia," *Evangelical Review of Theology* 31 (2007) 221–38 and "Practices of an Australian Baptist Intentional Community: Holy Transfiguration Monastery," *Cistercian Studies Quarterly* 42 (2007) 377–401. Another article will appear in *Baptist Quarterly* in 2008.

ONE

The New Monasticism

INTRODUCING THE NEW MONASTICISM

Monasticism is not specifically Christian, yet Christian monasticism has existed since the beginnings of Christianity. Christian monasticism has taken many forms, yet members of this diverse family of communities share many common characteristics. Most familiar is a rhythm of life: work, study, and set daily prayers; stability under a rule of life; a contemplative and sacramental lifestyle; and practices such as hospitality, simple living, and a sharing of economic resources with community members and with those in need beyond the walls of the monastery.

Today's new monastics are lineal descendants of earlier monastic generations. David Knowles, a Benedictine scholar, offers a biological analogy:[1] Members of a contemporary monastery may adapt their community to the needs of a particular setting or reject explicitly elements of the heritage, but they nonetheless manifest the DNA of their monastic forebears.

I have visited great Benedictine foundations like St. John's in Collegeville, Minnesota, or St. Benedict's nearby in St. Joseph, and older monasteries like the Trappist, or Cistercian Abbey of Gethsemani in Kentucky. I have also visited new monasteries that are modest in terms of numbers and resources, such as the Orthodox Monastery of St. John, north of Point Reyes Station near San Francisco, California, and several

---

1. Knowles, *Christian Monasticism*, 7–8.

monastic-like communities I discuss in this chapter—Iona in Scotland; Madonna House Apostolate in Combermere, Ontario; Little Portion near Eureka Springs, Arkansas; and the Caritas and Emmanuel House communities whose members live among and serve the poor in Memphis, Tennessee.

In each of the communities in this diverse family I have encountered a powerful witness to the Living Christ through compassionate service to others. All members of these communities might affirm words of Jubilee Partners in Comer, Georgia, "Jesus is Lord. Our life together is a response to the life, death, and resurrection of Jesus Christ. We joyfully order our lives in the belief that he calls us to love God and to love our neighbors as ourselves."[2]

In addition to a shared way of life, a sense of gratitude for the experience of God's love in Christ, and care of others, Christian monastics manifest a normal ebb and flow of institutional life. Monasteries are born, they grow, experience decline, and die. A few contemporary monasteries have a long history, such as Mar Saba in the desert of Judah, founded by St. Saba in 478, and Great Lavra on Mount Athos, founded in 963. However, these are exceptions rather than the rule. Hundreds, if not thousands, of monasteries that once flourished no longer exist.[3]

Related to this ebb and flow of institutional life, another common attribute of western Christian monasticism stands out. Over time, monastic practices tend to ossify. Vocations dry up. Then, every three or four hundred years, the Holy Spirit stirs up reform, renewed vitality, an increase in vocations, and sometimes, new orders.

In numerical terms, the phenomenon of monasticism has always been marginal. Especially today in secular, postmodern society, the new monastics have no voice, no sign from God, and no power to convince. They have only the journey that lies before them, the witness of their hearts, their lives of prayer and love, and a faith to move forward, as if always seeing the invisible.

Holy Transfiguration Monastery (HTM) grew in a Baptist congregation that began to take shape in 1869. Members write, "Our Community does not see Religious Life as a flight from the world, nor world denying

---

2. Mosley and Hollyday, *With Our Own Eyes*; Jubilee Partners, *Affirmation of Faith*.

3. Peifer, "Historical Reflections of the Life-Span of Monasteries."

or destroying. Religious Life is an injection of evangelical principles into the institutionalized structures of our age, both secular and religious."[4]

Recalling an earlier time when monastic renewal helped save western civilization, they see their journey, their vocation, "as a great mystery, something that in two thousand years no one has successfully defined. . . . [W]e must learn to be empty and quiet, making our journey, saying our prayers, always in the spirit of those who are poor."[5]

Intentionally countercultural, HTM members see themselves as offering church and society a path of hope and transformation. In a book that offers an incisive analysis of western culture, philosopher Alasdair MacIntyre observes,

> If my account of our moral condition is correct, we ought also to conclude that for some time now we too have reached that turning point. What matters at this stage is the construction of local forms of community within which civility and the intellectual and moral life can be sustained through the new dark ages that are already upon us. And if the tradition of the virtues was able to survive the horrors of the last dark ages, we are not entirely without grounds of hope. This time however the barbarians are not waiting beyond the frontiers; they have already been governing us for quite some time. And it is our lack of consciousness of this that constitutes part of our predicament. We are waiting not for a Godot, but for another—doubtless very different—St. Benedict.[6]

Whether or not another—doubtless very different—St. Benedict or St. Scholastica emerges or has already emerged since the period of World War II, horrors at least as grim as those of the last dark ages are upon us. Humanity faces challenges that threaten survival such as environmental degradation, epidemics, famine, human rights violations, terrorism, and war.

Ten years ago, Jonathan R. Wilson, who holds the Pioneer McDonald Chair in Theology at Carey Theological College in Vancouver, British Columbia, discussed the call of Alasdair MacIntyre for the construction of local forms of community within which life can be sustained through the new dark ages that are already upon us. Wilson wrote that we should

---

4. HTM, "Religious Life. Some Thoughts for the Journey," 1.

5. HTM, "Constitution," 1.

6. MacIntyre, *After Virtue*, 244–45.

pray, hope, and work for a form of life that would be continuous with the old monasticism in some respects, and discontinuous in other respects.

Wilson urged that Christians reverse the capitulation of the church to the Enlightenment project and return to the living tradition of the gospel. He outlined four marks that would be needed by a new movement to sustain faithful witness: a desire to heal the fragmentation of our lives in North American culture; a way for the whole people of God; discipline; and practices and virtues by which an undisciplined, unfaithful church might recover the discipline and faithfulness necessary to realize its mission in the world.

Wilson acknowledged that theological commitment and reflection must undergird a new monasticism. Right theology will not of itself produce a faithful church, which he characterized as the faithful living out the mission given to them by God in Jesus Christ, but that mission can be identified only by faithful theology. "So, in the new monasticism we must strive simultaneously for a recovery of right belief and right practice."[7]

Wilson was describing an insight that theological reflection informs practice; conversely, practices shape theological reflection. As in the Second Testament, following Jesus entails doing what he taught. "Just as I have loved you, you also should love one another. By this everyone will know that you are my disciples, if you have love for one another" (John 13:34–35). For Paul, faith was lifeless without love (1 Cor 13–14). For James, faith without works was dead (Jas 2:26). In the fourth century, Evagrius of Pontas wrote, "If you are a theologian, you will pray truly. And if you pray truly, you are a theologian."[8] Medieval Christians summarized in Latin, *lex orandi, lex credendi*, the law of prayer and belief.

Soon, Wilson's daughter and son-in-law, Leah and Jonathan Wilson-Hartgrove, helped found a new monastic community in Durham, North Carolina. Rutba House is one of a number of communities of Christians who think the church in western society has accommodated itself too easily to the consumerist and imperialist values of the culture. Responding to a call to enter more deeply into the pain of the world, many persons in the United States and elsewhere are on a journey similar to that of HTM, joining in prayer, simplicity of life, and service to the poor.

---

7. Wilson, *Living Faithfully in a Fragmented World*, 76.

8. Evagrius, "On Prayer," *Philokalia*, 1, 62, cited by HTM, "Beacons," 19.

In June 2004, Rutba House hosted a gathering of friends from around the country to discern the shape of a radical movement called the new monasticism. Out of the gathering came a book. Introduced by Jonathan R. Wilson, it offers strategic guidance for the movement. The new monasticism is diverse in form and characterized by these twelve marks:

1. Relocation to the abandoned places of Empire

2. Sharing economic resources with fellow community members and the needy among us

3. Hospitality to the stranger

4. Lament for racial divisions within the church and our communities combined with the active pursuit of a just reconciliation

5. Humble submission to Christ's body, the church

6. Intentional formation in the way of Christ and the rule of the community along the lines of the old novitiate

7. Nurturing common life among members of intentional community

8. Support for celibate singles alongside monogamous married couples and their children

9. Geographical proximity to community members who share a common rule of life

10. Care for the plot of God's earth given to us along with support of our local economies

11. Peacemaking in the midst of violence and conflict resolution within communities along the lines of Matt 18

12. Commitment to a disciplined contemplative life[9]

Participants in the network that has birthed the new monasticism are not unified by a shared theological tradition, or denomination, but by the wisdom of a shared legacy, and a vision of a spirituality that can shape the Christian life in postmodern society. This chapter briefly sur-

9. Rutba House, *School(s) for Conversion*, xii–xiii; the Rutba House Web site dedicates a page to the twelve marks of a new monasticism: http://www.newmonasticism.org/12marks/index.html; see also, Byassee, "New Monastics"; and Moll, "New Monasticism."

veys the legacy of Christian monasticism and stirring of the new monasticism. Three chapters, the heart of the book, present a case study of the
Community of the Transfiguration. A final chapter invites others grap-
pling with living in a world at risk to a journey of community, contemplation, and true personhood.

SURVEYING THE HISTORY OF CHRISTIAN MONASTICISM

During the early centuries after the death of Jesus, followers of Jesus
Christ often died for their faith. With the conversion of the Roman
emperor Constantine early in the fourth century, the era of the martyrs
ended. Everyone was a Christian. Christianity was legal and conversion
of Christians to Judaism or to another religion was illegal. Two specific
matters would prove disastrous in the history of Jewish-Christian relations. First, the Roman Catholic Church forbade clergy from charging
interest, a rule extended in the fifth century to the laity but not to Jews.
Also, Constantine supported the separation of the date of Easter from the
Jewish celebration of Passover. In a letter after the First Council of Nicea,
he stated,

> it appeared an unworthy thing that in the celebration of this most
> holy feast we should follow the practice of the Jews, who have im-
> piously defiled their hands with enormous sin, and are, therefore,
> deservedly afflicted with blindness of soul. . . . Let us then have
> nothing in common with the detestable Jewish crowd; for we have
> received from our Saviour a different way.[10]

Official recognition did not necessarily lead Christians to manifest
costly discipleship. But some Christians formed a special class of "holy
men and women." The *abbas* and *ammas* filled the wilderness areas of
Egypt, Syria, and the Holy Land. The desert saints lived on the margins
of thinly Christianized society and sought to grow in Christ-likeness
without interference from ecclesial or secular authorities. In this sense,
the early Christian monks were perfectly free of ties. In imitation of Jesus
during his earthly life, and in search of wholeness, solitude, union with
Christ, and salvation, they lived alone and apart from organized settlements. They resisted efforts by the institutional church to domesticate the
movement to the desert. They were determined virtuosos, ferociously independent, spiritual ombudspeople, icons or images of the living Christ.

10. Eusebius, *Life of the Blessed Emperor Constantine*, 3.8 (129).

They prayed, studied scripture, fasted, and subjected their bodies to extreme neglect and punishment.

In another sense, the desert saints lived in symbiotic relationship with Christians in the world. Able to offer healing, spiritual guidance, or prayer, they were professionals dependent for their survival, in some measure, on offerings from the wider community. Although in one sense the desert saints had abandoned the world, they nonetheless supported those they had left behind by acts of compassion and by holding their contemporaries in the Light of God's love. In words of an ancient source:

> assistance flows from their bones to all creation.
> Civilization, where lawlessness prevails,
> is sustained by their prayers.
> And the world, burdened by sin,
> is preserved by their intercession.
> The earth, heaving with controversy,
> is upheld by them.
> Troubled with speculation,
> their vigil fills it with calm.[11]

For both the eastern and the western monastic traditions, the exemplar of holiness *par excellence* was Anthony (251–356). Immediately after the great hermit's death, a *Life of Anthony* appeared. Ascribed to Athanasius of Alexandria, it was soon available in Latin translation. Around 386, Augustine of Hippo, then a teacher of rhetoric in Milan, heard about the saint from Ponticianus, an imperial official from Augustine's homeland in North Africa. Augustine had been studying Paul. When Ponticianus realized that Augustine had never heard about Saint Anthony, he was very surprised. Ponticianus described the story in great detail, and motivated Augustine to read the *Life of Anthony*.

The book made an enormous impression on Augustine. As he probed the depths of his being, he was moved to follow Anthony's example. Especially challenging for Augustine was Anthony's response to these words of Jesus, "If you wish to be perfect, go, sell your possessions, and give the money to the poor, and you will have treasure in heaven; then come, follow me" (Matt 19:21 and parallels).

11. Pseudo-Ephraim, *On Hermits and Desert-Dwellers*; cited in Brown, *Rise of Western Christendom*, 119. In *Contemplation in a World of Action*, Thomas Merton affirms the openness of contemplatives to the renewal of life in the Spirit for those in the world.

Immediately, Augustine recalled Paul's admonition to "put on the Lord Jesus Christ, and make no provision for the flesh, to gratify its desires" (Rom 13:14). "For in an instant as I came to the end of the sentence, it was as though the light of confidence flooded into my heart and all the darkness of doubt was dispelled."[12]

While Anthony's hagiographer provided one path followed by monks of third- and fourth-century Christianity, another path also emerged. Cells that the first hermits occupied became undesirable because they were too close to civilization. Monks began to move farther away from towns and villages. They began to gather in settlements. The communities were economically associated with nearby population centers, but the driving energy of the new monasticism was a movement outward, centrifugal in intention and missionary in outcome.

By organizing monastic communities, Pachomius of Egypt (286–346), a rough contemporary of Anthony, and Basil of Caesarea in the Holy Land (329–379), sought to bring order to this new development. To give shape to a new ideal, Pachomius wrote a rule that contained directions for all aspects of the monastic life. While the hermits of the desert had stressed chastity and poverty as essential ascetic practices, Pachomius added obedience to an abbot or abbess and stability as conditions of monasticism.

In the Christian east, numbers swelled. In the west, monasticism existed in a few small communities. After raids that began in 406, the Roman peace ended. The west fell apart and became a patchwork of separate regions. As the ancient Roman Empire disintegrated in the face of invasion by so-called barbarian tribes, monasteries offered security for monks and a nucleus for the villages and towns that grew up around the monastic complexes. Under God's protection, monks sought to live in conformity with the Gospel. Those who persevered would be united with Christ mystically in this life, waiting for that time when "the kingdom of the world has become the kingdom of our Lord and of his Messiah" (Rev 11:15).

Within three centuries or so, the earliest Christian monastic impulse began to ossify. In the west, at a time of social collapse, Benedict of Nursia, a small town north of Rome, became the instrument by which the Holy Spirit engendered the first reform in the cycle identified earlier.

---

12. Augustine *Confessions* 8.6 and 8.12; Brown, *Rise of Western Christendom*, 43.

Benedict lived around 480 to 547 CE. He went to Rome for his education but very quickly abandoned his studies and lived as a hermit for several years in a cave at Subiaco. Over time, he acquired a reputation for holiness and for his ability to heal or perform other miracles. Attracting many followers, he established several communities, including a monastery at Monte Cassino. There, outside Rome, he drew from the Bible and other sources to write a *Rule* (*RB*). When he died, he was buried beside the grave of Scholastica, co-foundress of the Benedictine order and his biological sister who preceded him a few years in death.

Living under the *RB*, monks were to follow Christ in obedience to the authority of an abbot, abbess, or another leader such as a prior or spiritual director. To be worthy of the task of governing a monastery, an abbot or abbess must always remember that he or she holds the place of Christ in the community (*RB* 2.1). The authority of an abbot, abbess, or other person in authority is limited only by the idea of the love of fathers and mothers for their children, treating all equally and caring for them as a shepherd cares for a flock.

Tim Otto is Associate Pastor of the Church of the Sojourners, a new monastic community located in San Francisco, California. From the immediacy of personal experience, he observes that obedience has been hard in every age, but that the simple wisdom of this area of monastic spirituality is potentially the toughest hurdle for modern people. Why did Benedict see obedience as so essential? He saw obedience as the way to God.[13]

The *RB* established a daily rhythm of prayer, work, and sacred reading. The cycle of prayer begins before sunrise and ends around sunset: matins (the morning office) followed by time for personal reading and prayer; lauds followed by community mass and breakfast; terce followed by work until noon; sext followed by a main meal and time for personal reading, prayer, and perhaps a siesta; none followed by chores and personal reading and prayer; vespers; supper; compline after which members of the community retire for the night.

For Benedict, physical work not only allowed monks to provide for their own livelihood, but also entailed an understanding that when monks worked, the sisters and brothers would be participating in God's

---

13. Otto, "Obedience," in Stock, *Inhabiting the Church*, 57; Sophrony, *Monk of Mt. Athos*, 53.

own work of creating and renewing earth. "When they live by the labor of their hands, as our [forebears] and the apostles did, then they are really monks" (*RB* 48.8).

As a spiritual practice for growing into Christ-likeness, Benedict mandated that monks should be steeped in the reading of Scripture. Benedict provided for silent, private reading of the Bible. Cultivating a listening attitude, monks were to follow the pattern of Jesus, who withdrew at times for prayer. Monks were to do so as well. During times of solitude, they were to wait on God and listen to God. "O that today you would listen to [God's] voice! Do not harden your hearts . . ." (*RB*, Prologue citing Ps 95:7b–8a). Benedict also designated times for corporate reading of Scripture. Monks were to undertake such reading quietly, slowly, and meditatively.

Benedict called poverty, community, humility, and other monastic practices "instruments of good works." By observing them, Benedictine sisters and brothers could attain to "the perfect love [that] casts out all fear" (*RB*, 7, 67, quoting 1 John 4:18). Contemporary Benedictine sister Joan Chittister has observed that Benedict was intent on developing people who want to live a sanctified life and therefore must change and embrace the world.[14]

In many areas, such as concerning the removal of a corrupt or heretical abbot or abbess, establishing new foundations, or the relationship between lay brothers and sisters and ordained priests, the *RB* was silent. One consequence was that, over time, those whose lives are ordered by the *RB* had to be flexible and open to innovation.

Benedictine monasteries drew people together from all classes of society. Self-contained homes for spiritual brothers or sisters, primarily lay people seeking God, Benedictine monasteries became centers of culture, education, pilgrimage, prayer, and the copying and transmission of sacred texts. Moderate in lifestyle and faithful to the traditions of the desert, the *RB* had an impact in Europe and ultimately around the world that is rivaled by few documents in Christian history. As an institution, Benedictine monasticism has proved almost unique for its durability over fifteen centuries.

By the year 800 CE, *RB* had achieved such authority that a new Holy Roman Emperor, Charlemagne, asked if any Rule other than that

14. Chittister, *Rule of St Benedict*, 153.

of Benedict existed.[15] In fact, other forms of monasticism were thriving in the west. In Cornwall, Wales, and Ireland, monasticism of a radically different type had captured the enthusiasm of entire populations. It often happened that when a Celtic king or chief became a Christian, he also became a monk, and took with him the whole clan. The Celtic monks had more in common with the desert saints, who had severe penitential practices, little organization, and no common rule such as that which Benedict provided his spiritual children. During the eleventh and twelfth centuries in western Europe, a reformed papacy and renewal of the great monasteries fueled another time of renaissance. This was a period of demographic growth, economic and commercial expansion, an increase of papal government, and a revolution in worldview. People were on the move to pilgrimage sites, castles, and monasteries, to new mission fields being opened by the crusaders against infidels and heretics, and to burgeoning towns and cities.

Crucial to this time of revival was the recovery of ancient spiritual sources. Ironically, this was a positive outcome of the crusades that brought Christians into contact with Islamic learning. In addition to returning from the Holy Land with manuscripts that had been lost to western Christians, the crusaders also introduced Islamic science and architecture to the west.

At the height of their glory, Cluny, Gorze, Moissac, and other Benedictine abbeys went through a period of re-established discipline, correction of abuses, and restoration of the spirit of the *RB*. Nonetheless, many felt that the reforms did not go far enough, which led to polemical attacks by some contemporaries, notably the upstart Cistercians who left Molesme for a "desert" called Cîteau in what is now southeastern France.

The Cistercian reform began in 1098. The first Cistercians called for a more thorough return to the characteristic practices or lifestyle set forth in the *RB* such as simplicity, humility, poverty, and silence. The new Cistercian abbeys provided western society with a positive body of religious teaching concerning holiness and salvation. As a social and economic phenomenon, monks were significant bulwarks of society. Among other roles, they were arbiters in political and ecclesiastical matters, pro-

---

15. See the entry on "Benedictines" in the online *Classic Encyclopedia*: http://www.1911encyclopedia.org/Benedictines (accessed December 14, 2007).

ducers, consumers, and missionaries. The monasteries were a great cultural force, with a virtual monopoly in matters of learning, interpretation of the Bible, music, architecture, aesthetics, and worship.

In his study of monastic culture in medieval Europe, the Benedictine scholar Jean Leclercq highlighted the contribution of the Benedictine tradition in shaping an "integral humanism" rooted in a desire for God and love of learning.[16] According to Leclercq, the medieval monks proved that the reading of Scripture and Christian contemplation did not lead to a flight from the world, but to humility, faith, and putting all that is beautiful, true, and good in human knowledge to the service of God in the world.

In Christian history, the era of monastic domination in the cultural, economic, intellectual, political, and spiritual arenas came to a predictable end. By the start of the thirteenth century, stagnation set in. Benedictines, including the Cistercians, ceased to be the main spiritual agents of society in the west. And then, again with inevitability, western Europe witnessed reform of the Benedictine tradition. In 1417, at a synod of monks sponsored by the Council of Constance (1414–1418), provision was made for the Benedictines to return to more strict observance of the RB. Two centuries later, the Cistercians underwent a similar time of reform. One of its principal architects, Armand de Rancé (1626–1670), abbot of La Trappe, engendered a new branch within the Cistercian family known as the Trappists.

The Carmelites illustrate the cycle of generation, stagnation, and reformation every three or four centuries. New monastic families, the original Carmelites were hermits who settled on Mount Carmel in the Holy Land where the prophet Elijah had lived in Biblical times. In 1204, they received a rule that expressed a calling "to meditate day and night on the law of the Lord and to watch in prayer."

By the sixteenth century, the order had lost a sense of its original vision. In Spain, Teresa of Avila (1515–1582) began to reform the order. A horse once threw her, and she landed in a mud puddle. When she complained about her ordeals, a voice from within her said, "This is how I treat my friends." She responded, "Yes, my Lord, and that is why you have so few of them."

16. Leclercq, *Love of Learning and Desire for God*, 179.

In the face of enormous hostility, Teresa established the so-called Discalced (barefoot) Carmelite order. Her spiritual director, John of the Cross (1542–1591) supported her in this work. Seventeen of the 32 monasteries she founded were convents of nuns. In 1970, the Catholic Church named her a Doctor of the Church, the first woman so recognized.[17]

Today in the United States, the Discalced Carmelite Nuns live as hermits in sixty-six Discalced Carmelite Monasteries. As well, there are friars and contemplative institutes such as the Nada Hermitage in Crestone, Colorado, where laity, married retreatants included, share in the charism of the hermits by praying, participating in the liturgies, and exploring through artistic and scholarly pursuits an embodied mysticism sensitive to ecological concerns.[18]

At least one monastic body escaped the ebb and flow I have just described. The Carthusians, half hermits, half communal monks, had grown slowly in France, and at the end of the twelfth century had adopted the constitution of an order, with annual general chapter, regular visitations, and the presidency of the prior of the Grande Chartreuse. Between 1350 and 1550, a period when other orders declined, the Carthusians thrived in the Low Countries, Rhineland, Italy, and England. Small in numbers but significant in the quality of its members, the order has remained to the present almost unchanged in observance. Carthusian monks exercise influence disproportionate to the size of the order by offering spiritual direction, notably in urban rather than rural settings. The only Charterhouse in North America is located in Arlington, Vermont.[19]

In the later middle ages, two Dutch reformers, Thomas à Kempis (ca. 1379–1471) and Desiderius Erasmus of Rotterdam (ca. 1466–1536) led a significant urban movement. À Kempis was a member of the Congregation of the Common Life and probably wrote the *Imitation of Christ*, an influential devotional manual. Erasmus was a prominent humanist. Large numbers of lay people in search of personal holiness and a mystical encounter with God shared a "modern devotion." Eisenach reformer Jakob Strauss described the radical love of these lay Christians

17. Ellsberg, *All Saints*, 448–50.

18. http://www.ocd.pcn.net/ocd/n2_usa.htm; former Crestone postulant Neyle Sollee, interview by Paul Dekar, March 17, 2007.

19. Knowles, *Christian Monasticism*, 122–23. For details, http://www.chartreux.org/en/frame.html. A prize-winning film, *Into the Silence*, depicts life at a contemporary Swiss Charterhouse.

who participated in the renewal of the fifteenth and sixteenth centuries as follows:

> Christ wants a community based on faith and every good work. . . .
>
> Christ requires no money for entrance into the community of the saints, only faith, hope, and love. . . .
>
> Christ wants people to give what they do not need for their own upkeep to the needy poor who cannot fend for themselves. . . .
>
> Christ wants the hungry fed. . . .
>
> Christ wants us to avoid drunkenness and gluttony. . . .
>
> Christ wants the naked clothed. . . .
>
> Christ wants the poor housed. . . .
>
> Christ wants us to lend and share with the poor without expectation of repayment. . . .
>
> Christ wants all Christians to have hearts aglow with faith.[20]

This passage reflects a broad impulse within early Protestantism. Matthew 25:31–45 and the Beatitudes as recorded in Matt 5:3–11 and Luke 6:20–22 inspired words from Menno Simons, for a time a Catholic priest and one of the first Anabaptists in Holland. Menno insisted that Christians must scrupulously follow the teachings of Jesus in every respect. True evangelical faith cannot lie dormant. It feeds the hungry. It provides something to drink to those who are thirsty. It welcomes the stranger. It clothes the naked. It brings healing to those who are sick. It visits those in prison. It comforts the sorrowful. It serves those that harm it. It shelters the destitute. It binds up those who are wounded. In short, it becomes life-giving sustenance to everyone. [21]

ANABAPTIST, BAPTIST, AND PIETIST STIRRINGS

Monastic antecedents dot Anabaptist, Baptist, and German Baptist (Brethren) history. While some stirred radical reform earlier, this family of Christians dates to January 21, 1525, when George Blaurock (ca. 1491–1529), Conrad Grebel (1498–1526), and others came to a new understanding of faith and grace in baptism while worshipping in a Zurich

20. Ozment, *Reformation in the Cities*, 84–85; Jackson, *New Schaff-Herzog Encyclopedia*, 122.

21. Menno, *Complete Writings*, 307.

home. Wanting to profess faith and repent of sin, Blaurock asked Grebel to baptize him. Grebel did so.

To bring cohesion to the movement, several Anabaptists gathered at Schleitheim on the Swiss-German border in 1527. They agreed to the *Schleitheim Confession*. For his role as a principal author of this document, onetime Benedictine prior Michael Sattler, who was born around 1495, was burned at the stake in May 1527.

The *Schleitheim Confession* expressed a consensus in seven areas. These were believers' baptism upon confession of faith; the practice of mutual church discipline (the ban); celebration of a Lord's Supper rather than the Mass; separation from evil in the world; the role of shepherds, rather than priests; rejection of the sword; and rejection of oaths.[22] Eventually, the movement developed into several bodies, several of which have maintained a strong communal basis, notably, the Amish, Bruderhof, Doukhobors, Hutterites, and Old Order Mennonites.

As a distinct reform movement, the Anabaptists sprang up wherever the Bible was translated into the vernacular, distributed, and read by small communities that tried actually to live what they found in the Word of God. There were never many Anabaptists. Catholics, Protestants, and various authorities made sure of that. But efforts to snuff out the movement failed. Anabaptists found shelter wherever they could. Many new monastics claim their ancestry from this left- or radical-wing of the sixteenth-century Protestant reformation.

As a movement distinct from, though influenced by, the Anabaptists, the Baptists emerged first in England during the first decades of the seventeenth century. They pressed such beliefs as justification by grace through faith, the authority of scripture, and the priesthood of believers to more radical conclusions. They called for religious liberty. They asserted that Christ alone was head of the church. They often met in homes. They opposed religious taxation. They went to prison for their convictions. They even elected "she-ministers" as pastors.

Early in the eighteenth century in Germany, Anabaptist and Baptist convictions shaped a movement known as pietism. "Dunkers" and "Brethren" observed believers' baptism and coupled the Lord's Supper with footwashing in a meal known as the love feast. Radical in disciple-

22. *Schleitheim Confession*, 10–18; Williams, *Radical Reformation*, 181–85.

ship, these forebears of the new monastics rejected oaths, evangelized energetically, and suffered for their non-resistant or pacifist convictions.

As descendents of this family of Christians, HTM members especially recall Ephrata, ancient name of Bethlehem, a German Baptist community that began in the eighteenth century in Lancaster County, Pennsylvania, as well as orders of Baptist sisterhoods, or deaconesses, that have grown up in Kenya[23] and in Germany.[24]

Regarding the latter instance, there are still convents in Berlin and Hamburg—Diakoniewerk Bethel and Diakoniewerk Tabea, respectively. Though they struggle with the aging of members and with not receiving new, younger members, these are living communities with active ministries. Both of them share the autonomy of Baptist free-church or congregational polity and do not follow a set liturgy. A third sisterhood in Hamburg, Albertinen Diakoniewerk, has just celebrated one hundred years of ministry. It has changed from a sisterhood to a mixed community with single female and male members as well as families.

New Stirrings

In recent times in the west, the Holy Spirit has guided many Christians to explore contemplative practices suited to the multiple complex contexts in which they live.[25] From personal visits to a number of spiritual centers, I note three signs that we are in a period of renewed monastic spirituality.

One has been the growth of lay associations that render more porous the wall that often has separated monastery and world. Generally, and in every Christian body, life-professed monks live contiguously in some form of enclosure: an abbey, a cloister, a collection of houses, or even a single dwelling. Few monasteries are to the degree that monks have little or no contact with the outside world, especially their families.

Thomas Merton anticipated this development. Coming to regard monasticism as a yes to the world, Merton encouraged many people to explore new forms of communal living. He saw contemplation as a way

---

23. Webb, "Protestant Sisterhoods."

24. Diakoniewerk Bethel Berlin, www.dgbethel.de; Diakoniewerk Tabea Hamburg, www.tabea.de; Albertinen Diakoniewerk Hamburg, www.albertinen.de.

25. Bass, *Practicing Congregation*, 61.

by which ordinary people might fulfill their calling as children of God. In a manuscript written in the 1950s, he noted,

> The most significant development of the contemplative life "in the world" is the growth of small groups of men and women who live in every way like the laypeople around them, except for the fact that they are dedicated to God and focus all their life of work and poverty upon a contemplative center.[26]

For Catholics, the reforms of Vatican II (1962–1965) have given impetus to many changes. Notably, the decrees on renewal of religious life and on the apostolate of lay people have led communities that had existed almost independent of other recognized institutions to come to terms with a new world of lay vocations and more porous boundaries.

In North America, traditional vocations may be declining, but some orders are growing. The number of Benedictine *oblates* has multiplied by over 75 percent over the past ten years. Lay vocations now outnumber traditional vocations by over ten to one.

As indicated in the introduction, the word *oblate* means a willingness to offer oneself in service to God and neighbor through a particular monastery without abandoning one's lay vocations. By integrating the rhythm of prayer, study, and work within their chosen way of life, oblates manifest Christ's presence in society. Single or married, they seek to live the teachings of Christ as interpreted by St. Benedict and in association with a specific Benedictine community. They often live close in geographic proximity to the monastery. This allows them to participate in the liturgies, monthly gatherings, or an annual retreat. This contributes to a widening and deepening of religious commitment.[27]

Parallel movements are taking place in other orders. Worldwide, there are now more than seven hundred thousand lay Franciscans and laity associated with Cistercian monasteries for whom "the Cistercian charism is a gift of the Holy Spirit bestowed not solely on those who live within monastic enclosures. Rather, we feel it is the gift of a 'way of life' that can be as appropriate for a layperson living in the world as it is for a monk or a nun living in a monastery."[28]

26. Merton, *Inner Experience*, 142.

27. Kulzer, "Monasticism beyond the Walls," 5; Talbot, "Call to a Modern Monastic Movement."

28. Eleven Lay Associates, "A Lay Response." 235–36.

A second sign of monastic renewal is the vitality of Protestant monasticism. This is noteworthy because many founders of the Protestant
churches, notably Luther, Calvin, Zwingli, and the Anabaptists, rejected
monasticism. Among the most prominent Protestant monastic communities in Europe are the sisters of Grandchamp in French-speaking
Switzerland, the brothers of Taizé in France, and the brothers of Bose in
Italy.

A third remarkable sign of monastic renewal is the emergence of the
new monasticism. These are intentional communities that draw on characteristics of the older traditions of monasticism. In the 1930s German
Lutheran theologian Dietrich Bonhoeffer (1906–1945) anticipated the
current of monastic renewal in a letter to his brother, Karl-Friedrich.

> I think I am right in saying that I would only achieve true inward
> clarity and sincerity by really starting work on the Sermon on the
> Mount. Here alone lies the force that can blow all this stuff and
> nonsense sky-high, in a fireworks display that will leave nothing
> behind but one or two charred remains. The restoration of the
> Church must surely depend on a new kind of monasticism, hav-
> ing nothing in common with the old but a life of uncompromis-
> ing adherence to the Sermon on the Mount in imitation of Christ.
> I believe the time has come to rally men [people] together for
> this.[29]

Bonhoeffer drafted a proposal for a community house and fleshed out
what he understood by a new monasticism. Those called to communal
life would find strength and liberation in service to the community, to
those in need, and to the truth. An alternative seminary for leaders of the
Confessing Church, the "House of the Brethren" offered a radical witness to a culture in which discipleship was difficult, if not impossible. Its
premature dissolution led to publication of a little booklet entitled *Life
Together*, which remains a powerful tract for our time.[30]

THE IONA COMMUNITY

Iona is a small island off the west coast of Scotland. Over centuries,
thousands of people have journeyed to the island as a place of pilgrim-

29. Letter of January 14, 1935, *Gesammelte Schriften* 3, 25, cited by Bethge, *Dietrich
Bonhoeffer*, 380.

30. Bethge, *Dietrich Bonhoeffer*, 385–86.

age. In 563, Columba founded a Celtic monastery that was a center of spirituality and evangelism. In the later middle ages, it was the site of a Benedictine Abbey. Early in the twentieth century, island residents restored the cathedral.

The Reverend George MacLeod, a parish minister in Glasgow, Scotland, founded the Iona Community in 1938. In those difficult days of the global economic depression, MacLeod felt seminarians needed more intimate contact with the poor. He brought together students and the unemployed or working poor. The group's first task was to restore the ruined monastic buildings of the abbey. The group began to attract male laity and then women and families. Over time, it established a house in Glasgow; two centers on Iona, where people could meet for prayer, common meals, and discussion; and Camas, a summer camp for young people on the nearby island of Mull.

Since 1952, the Iona Community has been under the auspices of the Church of Scotland. But its membership is open to members of other Christian denominations, and it has always welcomed people to its centers on Iona and Mull regardless of faith or tradition. The Iona Community understands itself as an ecumenical Christian community committed to seeking new ways of living the Gospel in today's world. Creative work in music and liturgy has flourished, creating a bond among members who eventually spread around the world.

True to concerns of the founder, Iona members continue both ecumenical work with the poor or exploited, and recovery of the deep spirituality of Celtic monasticism. Each year between March and December, over one hundred thousand visitors come to the island, with hundreds staying for a week as guests in various programs. The Iona Community maintains a resident group to welcome retreatants. Some residents are professed members of the Iona Community; others are volunteers sharing the practices of the wider community in a rhythm of work, worship, and recreation. They are joined by many unpaid assistants, who usually come to the community for two months, but sometimes for a longer period.

At present, the Iona Community is a dispersed community with a residential component. Some 250 members, men and women, lay and ordained, work in different jobs and live in many countries, though mostly in the United Kingdom. Members meet regularly throughout the year in local groups and in four plenary gatherings, including a week each year on Iona to renew their commitment to the community. As well, there

are over fifteen hundred Associates and fourteen hundred Friends worldwide. All are bound together by a five-fold rule of prayer, Bible study, accountability in the use of time and of money, and work for peace, justice,
and the integrity of creation.

In a history of the Iona Community, Ron Ferguson characterizes
it as an expression of a genuine Christian radicalism. Reflecting on the
contemporary spirit of community, he writes, "The testimony of so many
on Iona is that healing comes through living the questions, and not accepting easy answers. Somehow, the Church at large must work at ways of
restoring real community to its heart, and intentional communities such
as Iona can offer hard-won experience in the quest for such an essential
recovery."[31]

MADONNA HOUSE APOSTOLATE

In Canada, the Madonna House Apostolate grew from the ministry of
Catherine de Hueck Doherty (1900–1985). During the Russian revolution, she and her husband Baron Boris de Hueck fled with their newborn
son to Canada. These were troubled years for their marriage. Boris was
hired by a company in Montreal, Quebec, while Catherine began to get
many requests to lecture about her escape from communism. Later, as
they continued to go along separate ways, they divorced.

At the peak of her success as a public speaker, Catherine felt the
force of the verse "If you wish to be perfect, go, sell your possessions, and
give the money to the poor, and you will have treasure in heaven; then
come, follow me" (Matt 19:21 and parallels). So, in 1930 she gave up her
worldly goods and moved into an apartment in a poor area of Toronto,
Ontario, where she was committed to living "the gospel without compromise." With the support of the archbishop, she established Friendship
House, a storefront center for the works of mercy.

With encouragement from Dorothy Day, whose Catholic Worker
house was operating on similar principles in New York City, Catherine
moved to Harlem, where she created a Friendship House as a place of
hospitality, interracial justice, and reconciliation. She provided spiritual
direction for people in the community and volunteers, including Thomas
Merton, who continued to correspond with Catherine after he entered

31. Ferguson, *Chasing the Wild Goose*, 173. The Iona Web site is http://www.iona.
org.uk/.

the Abbey of Gethsemani and contributed royalties to her ministry from some of his writing.

In 1943, Catherine married a journalist, Eddie Doherty. In 1947, they left New York City and, two hundred miles northeast of Toronto at Combermere, established Madonna House Apostolate. The spirituality of the community was eastern Christian. The Melkite-rite Catholic churches blend Catholic and Orthodox elements and permit married priests. In 1969, Eddie Doherty was ordained in this tradition.

Catherine Doherty expressed the spirit of the Madonna House Apostolate in a prayer, "Lord, give bread to the hungry, and hunger for you to those who have bread." She also wrote a distillation of the Gospel called the Little Mandate, which came to her throughout the years as a response to prayer from Jesus:

> Arise—go! Sell all you possess . . . give it directly, personally to the poor. Take up My cross (their cross) and follow Me—going to the poor—being poor—being one with them—one with Me.
>
> Little—be always little!—simple—poor—childlike.
>
> Preach the Gospel *with your life—without compromise*—listen to the Spirit—He will lead you. Do little things exceedingly well for love of Me.
>
> Love—love—love, never counting the cost.
>
> Go into the marketplace and stay with Me . . . pray . . . fast . . . pray always . . . fast.
>
> Be hidden—be a light to your neighbor's feet. Go without fears into the depth of men's hearts . . . I shall be with you.
>
> Pray always. *I will be your rest.*[32]

Like Iona, Madonna House Apostolate has developed leadership gifts in many members of the community. This has enabled the community not only to survive the passing of the founders, but also to grow. Today, it remains a place of prayer, retreat, and service for the rural poor. Under the authority of the bishop of the Catholic Diocese of Pembroke, Madonna House Apostolate is a "Public Association of the Christian Faithful" with more than two hundred members. They are men and women who are dedicated to loving and serving Christ. Living in community, they make

32. Doherty, *People of the Towel and the Water*, 8–9; emphasis in original. Doherty, *Fragments of My Life*. The Madonna House Web site is www.madonnahouse.org/.

the traditional monastic promises of poverty, chastity, and obedience. In addition to a few staff priests, there are more than 125 priests, bishops, and permanent deacons who identify with Madonna House and try to live its commitments wherever they serve.

LITTLE PORTION COMMUNITY

Part of a growing network of lay contemplative movements, Little Portion Community is located at Berryville, near Eureka Springs in north-west Arkansas. John Michael Talbot describes its beginnings in the 1980s as follows:

> It seemed like we were trying everything and achieving nothing, except with my music and books. . . . We were becoming bogged down, some even began to "fry" emotionally, because we were trying to do so much with so few people who were, at best, novices in this way of life. We were democratic to a fault—we even voted on what dog food to buy! There was no clear direction. Some wanted a more intense expression of religious life. Some wanted less discipline, and yet more freedom to go into town, or out to dinner, or to a movie even more frequently. Some sisters wanted a veil, and others did not. Likewise, there were differences of opinion among the brothers concerning the habit. Dissent began to erode the ranks of our already tiny community. We called ourselves a "hermitage." But in reality most of our members were living pretty undisciplined lives. . . . I used a very passive form of leadership, and hesitated to take proper authority as founder. Frankly, I was still very new to this way of life and simply didn't know how to lead yet.[33]

The group's lack of a rule was part of the problem, but creating such a rule was complicated by the members' varied commitments to celibacy or marriage. During this critical period, Talbot was agonizing over the community's lack of direction when, like a fresh spring breeze, Sister Viola Pratka came to Little Portion Community. An Incarnate Word nun from Victoria, Texas, she brought twenty-five years of religious life and training to Little Portion.

Assisted by Sister Viola, Talbot made the decision to grant married couples and single persons the same status as celibates in Little Portion

---

33. O'Neill, *Signatures: The Story of John Michael Talbot*, 175. The Little Portion Web site is http://www.littleportion.org.

Community. Subsequently, on February 17, 1989, they married. Though their marriage came as something of a shock to many, this was a logical development whereby the Holy Spirit was leading many Protestants as well as Catholics to live in the community. Brother John and Sister Viola became examples of radical living, whether in marriage or as single people, for those called to an integrated community of celibate, single, and married lifestyles. According to author Dan O'Neill, this integration, coupled with a return to the roots of monastic life, have made the Little Portion Community a possible source of renewal or reform for the wider church.[34]

In 1990, the Catholic Church granted Little Portion Community canonical status as a Public Association of the Faithful under the authority of the bishop of the Catholic Diocese of Little Rock, Arkansas. Because the community integrates traditional celibates as well as married couples and single persons open to marriage, an extensive review process preceded this conferral because the Catholic Church had grave reservations about so radical a community wishing to take traditional vows. In the end, the church granted canonical status only to the professed celibates and not to married couples and individuals in the community. However, Little Portion Community regards all professed members as equal in status. The crisis in traditional vocations may contribute to the church ultimately revising its understanding of religious vocations.[35]

Noteworthy developments include the purchase, in 1987, of an Episcopalian facility nearby at More Mountain. Now called the Little Portion Retreat and Training Center, it has attracted thousands of persons to conferences, meetings, and retreats led by a wide range of people. Experiencing growth through the 1990s to the present, Little Portion Community has stabilized at around forty members and over five hundred associates. A wider monastic infrastructure has also taken shape, with cell groups around the globe. Members have touched the lives of the poorest of the poor through works of mercy. Locally, members maintain a health clinic for the poor, visit convalescent homes, clean the homes of the elderly and the disabled, and work with supportive agencies such as the St. Vincent de Paul Society. Globally, Little Portion Community operates Mercy Corps International, an agency that works with partners to

34. Ibid., 195.

35. Mark Shipler and John Michael Talbot, interviewed by Paul Dekar, April 9, 2004.

airlift emergency supplies to devastated areas of the world. Members have served in Honduras, the Philippines, and Palestinian refugee camps.

THE CARITAS COMMUNITY, MEMPHIS

The Caritas Community grew out of the vocations of Onie Johns and Richard Bryant. In 1999–2000, they participated in a ten-month formation process with the Memphis School of Servant Leadership (MSSL). Modeled on the Church of the Saviour in Washington DC, MSSL members believe that the best context for a transforming relationship with Jesus is one that engages us in an inner journey of contemplation, prayer, and study, and an outward expression of that journey in service, lives of compassion, and the work for social justice. Servant Leadership courses and other community gatherings are intended to challenge and sustain a lifelong journey of faith and service. The MSSL has adopted the following statement of purpose:

> being transformed toward the image of Christ through spiritual discipline;
>
> compassionate and well-versed in the art of loving;
>
> well-grounded in committed community;
>
> committed to building relationships with persons who are poor, outcast and lost;
>
> committed to the transformation of the world through courageous and sacrificial living.
>
> Our vision is to sponsor servant leaders who renew the church as servant in the world and, in so doing, recall us to our vocation as "the repairers of the breach, and restorers of the streets to live in" (Isa 58:12).

At the end of the formation year, the MSSL sounded a call to radical discipleship. Johns and Bryant responded by creating an intentional, ecumenical community named *caritas* from the Latin word meaning "Love for all People." Supported by a mission group, they looked for a house in Binghampton, one of the city's poorest neighborhoods, into which they could move.

In 2000, the Caritas Community purchased a home at 2532 Everett Avenue. Johns and Bryant were the first to live at Caritas Inn. Other members of the mission group moved into the neighborhood. After a year, Bryant married and moved out. Johns still resides at Caritas Inn, joined by others at varying times. At the heart of its vision, the Caritas Community seeks to attract and nurture those who are called to live in community; to form relationships with neighbors and experience their joys, celebrations, and struggles; to help all people—not just Christians—to recognize how God is working in their lives; to assist members of the neighborhood open to empowering themselves; to identify and develop the leadership capabilities of the people; to assist in the spiritual transformation of the neighborhood; and to establish and encourage partnerships that will provide economic opportunities in the Binghampton neighborhood.[36]

Supported by a mission group, volunteers, interns, and others in wider networks, Caritas Community has received a tax status that has enabled it to raise funds as a charitable donation and to purchase three other homes. These provide stability for people who might not be able to afford adequate housing. The community has also helped to create a neighborhood center called Caritas Village. Supported by a separate mission group, Caritas Village opened in late 2006 as a place of hospitality offering food and a range of worship and artistic activity. Johns explains,

> Our goal at Caritas Village is to encourage creativity as a means of breaking down barriers between disparate community members. We believe that through artistic endeavors, children can discover their gifts and feel more empowered, walls of hostility between people who differ based on race and economic status can be diminished, and through their own passion, community artists can help positively transform an under-served, impoverished, inner-city neighborhood.[37]

EMMANUEL HOUSE COMMUNITY, MEMPHIS

In the summer of 2003, Bob and Sharon Gazaway and Pete Gathje and Jenny Case traveled from Memphis to Atlanta, Georgia, where they met with Ed Loring and Murphy Davis, founders of the Open Door Community. Pete had a relationship with the Open Door Community dating back to 1987. Out of these conversations, Bob and Sharon Gazaway, Pete Gathje, and Jenny Case developed a vision for creating a

---

36. Brochure, 2000. The MSSL Web site is www.servantleadership-memphis.org.

37. Keplinger, "It's All about Love"; Phillips, "Caritas Village."

similar community in Memphis. It would serve the poor and offer a morally coherent alternative to the dominant values of United States society as a whole. Called to follow Jesus, who is "God with us" (Emmanuel), they set forth their understanding in the following statement:

> Emmanuel House Community is a residential community in the Catholic Worker tradition. We seek to give each other mutual support in a life of discipleship and service. We share a life given to simplicity, reflection, prayer, nonviolence, and work that supports human dignity. We stand in solidarity with the poor and suffering of the world. We engage in hospitality for homeless persons, support for prisoners and their families, educational work in schools and the community, and efforts to abolish the death penalty. We resist racism, materialism, and militarism. We advocate for a more just society through nonviolent protests, grassroots organization, and the publication of our newspaper.[38]

As discussions progressed in early 2004, the group purchased a house at 51 North Auburndale Street, in midtown Memphis. By late June it was possible for Pete and Jenny to move into the upstairs while renovation of the ground floor took place. That September, upon completion of the renovations, Bob and Sharon moved in. Soon thereafter, community members began holding "prayerful reflection" each Sunday, Monday, Tuesday, and Thursday night and sharing evening meals on Sundays and Mondays.

By early November, the Emmanuel House Community had established a "common pot." This system enabled members to pool their incomes, cover household and personal needs, and fund the work of the community. Another couple joined, and volunteers began to support the ministries of the community.

Discerning a need on the part of men and women who regularly waited for work at a labor pool about half a mile from the house on North Auburndale, Emmanuel House Community initiated its first ministry outreach on December 6, 2004. That day, community members prepared and distributed thirty sack lunches to workers. Ever since, Emmanuel House Community members have continued to supply workers lunches. At the time of writing, they serve sixty-four workers at two labor pools each Monday morning.

38. Gathje and Case, "Emmanuel House Begins," 1. The Emmanuel House Web site is under construction.

Later that December, members of Emmanuel House organized a nonprofit organization, Emmanuel House Manna, which in 2006 received a tax exempt status that has enabled the community to raise funds for its various works of mercy and justice. In addition to the preparation and distribution of sack lunches, current activities of Emmanuel House Manna include providing coffee to drop-ins; transporting family members of a death row inmate to the prison for visits; hosting evenings of dinner and fellowship for inner-city youth; collecting donated goods; and helping maintain a place of hospitality for homeless and poor persons.[39]

The hub of the latter work is Manna House, which opened in October 2005 at 1268 Jefferson Avenue. In the words of Elizabeth Kruczek, "when we first saw it [Manna House], it was a wreck. After the purchase was complete, the transformation could begin. . . . we took down one of the old buildings to make room for something beautiful." Ever since, volunteers have been providing coffee on cold days, water for showers, and other expressions of hospitality that make Manna House feel like a home.[40]

Living at Emmanuel House, residents build community through prayerful reflection, Bible study, shared meals and decision making, works of mercy, and events organized in wider society, with other groups like the Tennessee Coalition to Abolish State Killing, with a focus on justice, peace, and the integrity of creation. At present, these activities include weekly vigils against the war in Iraq and the death penalty, and participating in public forums on issues, events, and campaigns as they arise. As members have explained, they seek to live by the gospel especially as it has been practiced in the spirit of the Catholic Worker Movement and those movements of intensive Christianity within the history of the church. Community members look to exemplars of the faith such as Benedict of Nursia, Francis and Clare of Assisi, Teresa of Avila, Dorothy Day, Martin Luther King Jr., Fannie Lou Hamer, Thomas Merton, Cesar Chavez, Oscar Romero, and Philip Berrigan for inspiration and guidance in their lives.

39. Bob and Sharon Gazaway, interviewed by Paul Dekar, March 16, 2007; Gathje and Case, "Emmanuel House Begins," 7–8.

40. Kruczek, "Birth of Manna House," 2, 4. When the author wrote this piece, she was eleven years old.

CONCLUDING REFLECTIONS

Monasteries and intentional communities have played several positive roles in eastern and western Christianity. Sometimes, monasteries have provided a place of safety, or even survival. Emerging at a time when the wider culture collapsed, Benedictine monasticism provides an example. However, monasteries cannot be regarded primarily as places of flight or withdrawal. The monastic life is not an option for someone trying to escape her or his problems.

Monasticism is highly countercultural. Monasteries, or monastic-like communities have at times been prophetic, witnessing to a culture in which discipleship has been difficult, if not impossible. The confessing church movement in Germany, with its clandestine seminary at Finkenwalde, offers an example.

Monasteries have also served the role of generating renewal. During recent decades, the reform of traditional monasticism within the Catholic and Orthodox traditions, the emergence of ecumenical monasteries rooted in the Protestant reform tradition, and the stirring of a new monasticism have provided new ways for sensitive and thoughtful people to live as Christians.

The idea of redeeming time is a way to understand what is happening to monasticism in the west early in the twenty-first century. Every four hundred years or so, Christian churches of the West have experienced an upsurge in monasticism. Today, if warnings about the effects of global warming and other environmental issues are fulfilled, we face possible collapse and subsequent transformation of civilization. The new monastics are preserving in postmodern, secular society not only a living tradition that has prospered in western society for nearly two millennia, but also a fresh vision of life's final meaning and a new spiritual direction by which an emerging generation of religious seekers may come into relationship with that meaning.

Communities such as Iona in Scotland; the Madonna House Apostolate headquartered at Combermere in Ontario, Canada; Little Portion Community near Eureka Springs, Arkansas; the Church of the Saviour in Washington DC and offspring such as the Caritas Community in Memphis, Tennessee; and the Catholic Worker movement with offspring such as the Emmanuel and Manna Houses in Memphis, Tennessee, are multiplying and influencing local neighborhoods.

What is happening has led observers of the contemporary religious scene in North America to characterize the new monasticism, or congregational monasticism, as a framework by which the "practicing church" can give Christians in general and those involved in intentional community a revolutionary way to live more faithfully, to resist such aspects of western culture antithetical to Christianity such as consumerism and greed, and to overcome the moral fragmentation of contemporary society. A growing body of literature has documented the radical love evident in the lives of members of these communities.[41] They have offered hope, healing, and a vision of life lived in fullness to those open to transformation by their witness.

The Gaelic idea of *grieshog*, or smooring the coals, is an especially apt description of this phenomenon. The idea is to keep a fire alive by burying the coals in order to keep them burning through the night and to have a fast-starting fire in the morning. Instead of cleaning out the hearth, the householder covers the coals without suffocating them.[42]

Monasteries represent a numerically tiny part of the Christian church. Their renewal around the world is occurring at a time of danger, need, and opportunity. Monastic culture is not a dying fire. Rather, traditional monks and a generation of new monastics are like burning embers. With warmth and compassion, these smoldering coals are encouraging people to listen, look, and see what God has provided for the good of humankind: our very being, beauty, food, people, music, land—in short, more than enough to give us life in abundance.

God wills that we live well. Do we ourselves care enough to be passionate about God's will for all living things, including every wetland, ocean, child, inner-city, woman, and moment of life? I believe so. The new monastics show us a way to live intensely, with enthusiasm, making straight in our dark times the way of our God (Isa 40:3).[43]

Carol Gilbert, O.P., is the author of the prayer with which I close this chapter. Having chosen the way of community, contemplation, and true personhood, Sister Gilbert was arrested in 2003 with two other Dominican sisters. Their alleged crime was to have trespassed on a nuclear weapons facility in Colorado where they had gone to pray for peace. In February

41. Wilson, *Living Faithfully*, 68–78; Bass, *Practicing Congregation*, 58.
42. HTM, "Testament and Pastoral Rule," 19.
43. Chittister, *Fire in These Ashes*, x; *Gospel Days*, 158.

2004, Sister Carol sent the following from prison as a testimony to the fruits of a radical love characteristic of the new monastics:[44]

> Close your eyes and you will see clearly.
> Cease to listen and you will hear truth.
> Be silent and your heart will sing.
> Seek no contact and you will find union.
> Be still and you will move forward in the tide of the Spirit.
> Be gentle and you will not need strength.
> Be patient and you will achieve all things.
> Be humble and you remain entire.

44. Rutba House, *School(s) for Conversion*, 171.

TWO

History of Holy Transfiguration Monastery

INTRODUCING THE COMMUNITY OF THE TRANSFIGURATION AND HOLY TRANSFIGURATION MONASTERY

The Community of the Transfiguration and Holy Transfiguration Monastery (HTM) began to take shape in the early 1970s. In 1972, Brother Graeme completed four years of study at the Melbourne Bible Institute and Whitley College, now a part of Melbourne College of Divinity. He spent nearly three years in the Community of the Glorious Ascension (CGA), founded in 1960. Brother Steve took leave from his studies in Michigan. He spent 1971–1972 on a Kibbutz in Israel before proceeding to England.

In 1973, Brother Graeme and Brother Steve met at Cleeve Priory, in Somerset, England, then the founding community, or mother-house, of CGA. The two brothers were at CGA at the height of its life and growing influence. The remaining members of CGA now live in the south of France and in Kingsbridge, in Devon, England.

Brother Graeme and Brother Steve were both drawn to monastic spirituality by a thirst for intimacy with God. Together at CGA, they explored the place of monasticism in Orthodox, Catholic, and Protestant spirituality. They read classic monastic sources such as Pachomius, Basil, the *Rule of Benedict* (*RB*), and *The Philokalia*, a collection of texts written between the fourth and fifteenth centuries by spiritual masters of the Orthodox Christian tradition. First published in Greek in 1782, *The*

Philokalia has exercised an influence far greater than that of any book in the recent history of the Orthodox Church other than the Bible.

Founders: front, left to right: Brother Os, Sister Diane, Brother Neil;
back, Brother Graeme, Brother Steve

In 1975, after two years together at CGA, the two brothers went their separate ways. Brother Graeme left for the United States, after which he returned to Australia. Brother Steve stayed in England and later immigrated to Australia.

Late in 1975, Brother Graeme returned home and accepted the interim pastorate at Norlane Baptist Church in a suburb of Geelong. By November 1976, four young people were gathering for contemplative prayer. They asked if, amidst a culture of materialism, they might model church as an honest reflection of the Holy Trinity and practice a kind of evangelism that identified with the poor in solidarity with the marginalized. Wanting a more authentic discipleship that reflected the deeper implications of their baptism, they began to explore forming a new monastic community. In typical Australian idiom, Brother Os urged, "Let's give it a go and see what happens." Thirty years later, the entire initial group remains together: Brothers Graeme, Os, Neil, Sister Diane, and Brother Steve who arrived to stay in 1986.

Since 1869, a Sunday school and home mission of the Baptist Union of Victoria had met at Breakwater, a suburb of Geelong. In the 1970s, the congregation was praying that God would bring new life. Breakwater Baptist Church welcomed the emerging Community as a mission group of the congregation. Congregation and Community began a journey together of deep mutual respect and cooperation. In the next few years, others came from Anglican, Baptist, Catholic, Pentecostal, and Uniting Church communions. Some Community members have changed denominations and become members of the Baptist congregation, though the Community has never required this.

In 1989, under a new constitution, members of Breakwater Baptist Church joined the Community. Having long expressed its commitment to seek to live in the light and love of the Transfigured One, members chose the name Community of the Transfiguration. In 2001, a revised constitution formally used the name Holy Transfiguration Community.

Presently, HTM has identified four possible Community lifestyles. One might live at the Cloister, as a member of a house of prayer or Skete, in the Greater Community, or less formally, as Companions in identification with HTM as a spiritual home. A common calling to contemplative prayer, simplicity, a Eucharistic focus, and the nurture of monastic spirituality binds Community members together.

Those who wish to join the Community indicate their intention by letter. Membership is not automatic; that is, not without periods of discernment and testing the call. Membership means a movement in very personal ways:

> from isolation to solitude
> from individualism to the personal
> from self to others
> from the corporate to community[1]

Life-professed members go through a period of formation of no less than seven years. When the membership of a Skete reaches twelve life-professed members, then it may be constituted as a monastery of the Community of the Transfiguration. However, the life of the Skete, if such numbers are not reached, remains an authentic and unique expression of the Community.

Beginning in 1997, Sister Miriam, a minister of the Uniting Church in Australia, maintained the Skete of St. John the Divine at Mt. Waverley, a suburb of Melbourne. In 2000, she moved to the Cloister, and the Skete at Mt. Waverley closed. Several who participated in the Skete have since traveled to Breakwater to join in the Community's liturgies and prayers.

As of 2007, eighteen life-professed monks live at Breakwater, the Cloister serving as a house of prayer. Five life-professed monks live in Melbourne and have formed St. Luke's House of Prayer, or St. Luke's Skete, as a constituent part of St. Luke's Baptist Community in the suburb of Abbotsford. Thirteen Greater Community members live in walking distance or a short drive from the Cloister. Seven others in the Greater Community are establishing Sketes in the United Kingdom, the United States, and Canada. They try to observe the rhythm of the Cloister, visit the Cloister every eighteen months, and manifest other signs of unity. The Companions, who have a simple discipline and visit the Cloister regularly, number in the hundreds.

HTM has influenced other communities in Australia, the United Kingdom, and elsewhere. One that sought out HTM members for their experience in trying to balance the challenges of being an integrated community of single persons and married couples, activists and contemplatives, is Peace Tree in Perth, Western Australia. Taking shape in

---

1. HTM, "Baptist Church in Breakwater, 1869–2001," 25.

2003, the Peace Tree Community has brought together students and young activists focused especially in the environmental movement and nonviolent peace activism. For example, Jarrod McKenna is creative director of Empowering Peacemakers in Your Community, an organization that seeks to equip a generation of eco-prophets in transformative nonviolence.

Since 2004, Peace Tree members have spent significant periods of time at Breakwater. As well, HTM members have journeyed to Perth. Offering retreats and spiritual direction, HTM members have encouraged this courageous group of young people as they have completed their studies and moved into careers.

COMMUNAL EXPERIMENTS IN AUSTRALIA

With varying degrees of success, Australians have a rich history of undertaking communal and utopian experiments. Only a few have lasted many years. Some have been Christian. For example, in 1852, some Lutheran immigrants founded Herrnhut on land near Hamilton, two hundred miles west of Melbourne. Named for the first Moravian community formed in Germany in 1722 on land belonging to Count Zinzendorf, Herrnhut was formed out of a utopian ideal of creating a better world. Over its thirty-seven year history, this remarkable group provided a safe haven for Aboriginal people, a refuge for homeless people, and arguably Australia's first women's shelter, all while efficiently managing a large farm and supporting, on average, about fifty people.[2]

Since the 1960s, many people have re-appraised economic, political, and religious structures and imagined a different shape for society. Many Australians are openly hostile to Christianity. This is due to a number of factors including the role of some Christians during the early history of the Commonwealth in the transport of convicts to Australia and in the harsh treatment of Aboriginal people. With Aboriginal Australians a possible exception, there is a great divide between institutionalized religion and postmodern life in general.

Bold, brash, and hedonistic, countless Australians say that religion is irrelevant. Yet many without formal religious affiliation are engaged in personal spiritual journeys.[3] In his study of modern spiritualities, David

2. Metcalf and Huf, *Herrnhut: Australia's First Utopian Commune.*

3. Porter, *Land of the Spirit?* 9–10.

Tacey, who teaches literature and Jungian psychology in Melbourne at La Trobe University, has found that many modern people turn to new connective technologies such as Internet, e-mail, and mobile phones to meet a felt need for community and spirituality. These new inventions do what they claim, at least at one level, but they fall short of addressing a malaise of modernity and, worse, a deeper crisis. He quotes artist and lay theologian Michael Leunig in his contention that rejection of formal religion has resulted in disequilibrium of the soul.

> We are in the midst of the pillaging and rape of the psychological ecosystem, the ecology of the soul. There's a great, delicate, inter-connected ecology that goes on in people's lives. We're defiling it, plundering it, exploiting it, and this will have tremendous conse-quences for the emotional health of society.[4]

Tacey concludes his analysis of the postmodern world with words from a popular song by U2, "I still haven't found what I'm looking for." Tacey expresses hope that in the future western people will overcome their modern obsession with imitation, stand-ins, substitutes, and copies, and develop a "deep real" that connects us to our invisible, life-sustaining roots.[5]

As a consequence of a deeply experienced yearning of the heart for community and an intimate experience of the universal love and power of God, experimental groups have abounded in Australia and around the world. According to William J. Metcalf, social historian at Griffith University in Brisbane, Queensland, and a member of the board of the International Communal Studies Association, over sixty thousand Australians were involved in an alternative lifestyle movement during the early 1990s. About a quarter of them lived in intentional communities.[6]

Dave Andrews has written about his experience with the House of Freedom, founded in 1972 in Brisbane, Queensland. The community had as a major focus Christian witness for peace and justice through direct nonviolent action.[7] More recently, he has been part of Waiters' Union in Brisbane. Andrews describes the vision of this intentional Christian community as follows:

---

4. Tacey, *The Spirituality Revolution*, 220.
5. Ibid., 225–26.
6. Metcalf, *From Utopian Dreaming to Communal Reality*, 39.
7. Andrews, *Christi-Anarchy*, 137.

a group of us feel called to stop, to look, to listen, and, above all, to wait. We want to wait on God, be aware of his presence, attentive to his purpose, and enter into his response to our area. We want to wait on our neighbours: not setting any agenda or setting up any agencies, just helping out in any way we can.

We have a dream. We dream of a world in which all the resources of the earth will be shared equally between all the people of the earth, so that even the most disadvantaged among us will be able to meet basic needs with dignity and joy. We dream of a great society of small communities cooperating interdependently to practice personal, social, economic and political compassion, love and justice, and peace.

We dream of people developing networks of friendships in which the pain we carry deep down can be shared openly in an atmosphere of mutual support and respect. We dream of people understanding the difficulties we have in common, discussing our problems, discussing the solutions, and working together for personal growth and social change in the light of the love of Christ.

We yearn to make this dream a reality in our own locality. . . .[8]

Introducing this book, I mentioned the House of the Gentle Bunyip, one of the intentional Christian communities to emerge in Australia during this period of ferment. The Bunyip began in 1975. In an inner suburb of Melbourne, Athol Gill (1937–1992), his wife Judith, and ten members of Clifton Hill Baptist Church identified five principles that would shape their common life.[9]

First, the community centered its devotion on Jesus Christ. Second, members acknowledged their dependence on God's grace and sought to share it with others. Third, the community existed for the sake of others, notably, "the little people of the world." Fourth, members understood community as a place where they could discover their God-given gifts, develop them, and use them within the context of the community's developing mission in the world. Finally, members did not take on a structure or a confession of faith that would bind them in the present and ultimately bury them in the past. They sought to live into a more faithful and authentic Christian discipleship.

8. Ibid., 171.

9. Gill, *Fringes of Freedom*, 91–92.

For twenty years, members of the Bunyip sought a radical revision of their lives and a revolutionary change in the structures of church and society. Living in community, members worked in areas such as housing, aged care, education, peace activism, care of the mentally ill, human rights, and policy issues such as public health, public housing, and gambling. Although he was committed to a co-operative style of leadership, Athol Gill had such an enormous influence as founder and wisdom-bearer that, when he died prematurely, the Bunyip could not navigate the transition and survived only six years. However, Clifton Hill Baptist Church in which the Bunyip had been housed continues as a neighborhood congregation.

On November 8, 1998, at the closing worship service, Rowena Curtis evaluated the impact of the community. By the time I finished this book, she had become pastor of Collins Street Baptist Church in Melbourne.

> The Bunyip had both a role and an influence in the Australian church and society. It birthed a range of mission projects, many well beyond Clifton Hill; it inspired a host of gospel scholars and urban missioners, both women and men across state borders; by its existence and through the writings of Athol Gill, it influenced a wide group of people to the ends of the earth. There is no doubt that the story and influence of the Bunyip will live on beyond today and beyond those of us who were part of it.[10]

Another group grew from the Dallas Baptist Church, formed in 1968 at Broadmeadows in the northern Melbourne suburbs. By 1974, charismatic and communitarian movements such as the Church of the Redeemer in Houston, Texas, had an influence on the congregation. Members established the Dallas Welfare and Youth Service and, in 1974, a community known as "Commonlife." Attracted to an intentional community marked by contemporary worship and ministry opportunities, new members joined. Through the 1990s, they offered a range of community services and small business ventures.

At least eight Christian communities active around Melbourne during the 1970s, under a variety of names—base church, intentional community, house church—have ceased to exist. What happened? Sometimes, conflict intruded. Sometimes, members succumbed to exhaustion. Thomas Merton cites writer and teacher Douglas Van Steere

10. Neville, "Completing the Story, Claiming the Heritage," 389.

(1901–1995) of the Religious Society of Friends to the effect that many peace activists succumb to the rush and pressures of modern life. Merton warns that to allow oneself to be carried away by a multitude of conflicting concerns, to commit oneself to too many demands, to undertake too many projects, and to want to help everyone in everything is to yield to a pervasive contemporary form of violence. More than that, it is cooperation in violence.[11]

In my experience, the frenzy of many peace activists neutralizes their own inner capacity for peace. It destroys the fruitfulness of their work because it kills the root of inner wisdom that makes work fruitful. In the cases of the Bunyip and Dallas communities, the core groups were highly focused outward. With few nurturing sources other than the mission itself, the communities became fragmented and hollow.[12] Desiring to be part of an intentional community with a contemplative focus, members of these two communities, as well as other communities that no longer exist, found their way to other intentional communities, among them St. Luke's Baptist Community and the Community of the Transfiguration.

St. Luke's Baptist Community[13]

St. Luke's Baptist Community is located in Melbourne's city core in Abbotsford. Members are committed to sharing together a life of prayer, celebration, hospitality, and service. As a Baptist congregation, St. Luke's Baptist Community has a history stretching back to the 1880s. It was originally formed as an outreach of the Collins Street Baptist Church, located in central Melbourne. Over its history, St. Luke's has had a strong focus on mission and outreach. In the 1940s, as Melbourne began to expand and its outer suburbs began to grow, the once-residential area of Abbotsford became a heavily commercialized and industrialized suburb.

During the 1980s the area began to undergo another transformation, with industry moving further out and families moving back in. However, urban change had taken a significant toll on the congregation,

11. Merton, *Conjectures of a Guilty Bystander*, 86.

12. Munro, "A History of the House of the Gentle Bunyip (1975–1990)," 106; Stephen Hammond, Naomi Hammond, and Olivia Hammond, interview by Paul Dekar, June 16, 2004; Mark Bailey, interviewed by Paul Dekar, June 22, 2005; Ann Lock, pastor of Brunswick Baptist Church in Brunswick and HTM Chaplain, interview by Paul Dekar, July 8, 2004.

13. Bailey, "St. Luke's Skete."

which greatly decreased in membership and in its ability to engage in program-based mission and outreach. A group of younger people formed around a small band of faithful people that remained committed to the local area and to the work of the congregation. This new group drew from two often-divergent streams of Australian contemporary culture at the time: the Charismatic and Social Justice Movements. However, the focus of this new group expressed itself in the development of an intentional residential community. Singles and married couples lived together, seeking a simpler, more authentic way of being the church.

Many of those who formed the community in the 1980s are still together and now form the basis of a group known as St. Luke's House of Prayer. The focus of this group is to live a life that is grounded in the monastic tradition of contemplative prayer and stillness.

Ecumenism has played a strong part in the outworking of the commitment of members of St. Luke's House of Prayer to mission. They are linked to the local neighborhood in which they live. They work ecumenically with other churches in the immediate area on issues of local, national, and international concern.

The community has undertaken a variety of locally based outreach specifically designed to build bridges of tolerance and understanding amongst people of different socio-ethnic backgrounds. With other congregations in the area, the community has developed a neighborhood gardening initiative, a family camping program, and a series of shared celebrations with local indigenous people. In this way, within a local and ecumenical context, members of St. Luke's House of Prayer have sought to incarnate their shared commitment to reconciliation and to nurture a greater sense of community amongst diverse groups of people.

Early in 2006, five members of St. Luke's House of Prayer developed formal links with HTM in Breakwater. At the start of Holy Week, the two communities recognized their ties officially. Sisters Gail, Kerri, and Alleyne and Brothers Mark and Eddie renewed their baptismal vows and received white monastic albs that distinguish the Community of the Transfiguration. The next night, the folk from Breakwater went to Abbotsford for a service at which they affirmed their ways of connection.

Community of the Transfiguration members of St. Luke's House of Prayer, or Skete, in Abbotsford and of the Cloister at Breakwater are committed to a way of life that finds its truest expression through the vocation of contemplative prayer. Living out of this calling, members of the expanding Community have grown into a new and greater sense of faith and connection, personally and collectively.

In much the same way that the process that culminated in publication of this book began without promise or expectation as to what would follow, every step of the journey taken so far has surprised members of St. Luke's House of Prayer and the Cloister. First as separate communities and now together as two expressions of the Community of the Transfiguration, members have been on a pilgrimage of discovery rooted in the love and compassion of a merciful, gracious, compassionate, and nonviolent God. The journey has transformed their understanding of incarnational mission and deepened their commitment to offering radical love. Brother Eddie describes the journey by saying, "The future is way open to us all, and in many ways we are not too sure of where it will take us all. But that is exciting!"

COMMUNITY OF THE TRANSFIGURATION

We now pick up in greater detail the story of the Community of the Transfiguration summarized briefly in the first section of this chapter. When Brother Graeme left England in 1975, he traveled around the United States before returning to Australia. Three places had a marked impact on the development of his thinking about community. One was the Church of the Saviour in Washington DC, which he has described as an indispensable model.

In the late 1940s, Gordon Cosby and a few others began the Church of the Saviour in Washington DC. As a basis for a life of discipleship, every able person involved with the Church of the Saviour participated in small groups. Generally, each group had no more than a dozen members, and each developed a set of practices common to members of the group. Based on a model they believe Jesus established during his lifetime, members of the Church of the Saviour held together their inward and outward journeys in creative tension. The journey inward entailed more interior disciplines such as prayer, meditation, and fasting. The journey outward entailed serving those on the margins of society.

During the 1970s, many churches adopted small groups for Bible study and fellowship. As a result, the Church of the Saviour asked for more commitment and required members to be part of a formation process through which they might grow in love for God, self, and others. Over time, this usually involved some kind of personal transformation. The Church of the Saviour encouraged participants in the mission groups to take their brand of radical discipleship back to the traditional church, rather than grow larger and more centralized. There was, however, a problem. No one ever wanted to leave![14]

By 1975 the mission groups were forming six congregations. Each had a primary focus, namely, housing (Jubilee), children (Seekers), hospitality (Potters House), polyculturalism (8th Day), public policy (Dunamis), and retreats (Dayspring).

Although Gordon Cosby of the founding generation has continued to preach for the last thirty years at an ecumenical service attended by many visitors, the Church of the Saviour now exists as a servant leadership network around North America. Faithful to the original vision of the Church of the Saviour, Christians have formed mission groups around areas like healthcare for the homeless (Christ House), neighborhood renewal (New Community), post-Alcoholics Anomymous recovery (Lazarus House), and the school of Servant Leadership (Festival Church). Each group develops its own style of worship, preparation for membership, and mission.

The level of commitment and emphasis on the inward/outward journey remains a common thread. The journey inward involves three engagements: with oneself, the path of self-knowledge and integration; with God, the path of fasting, meditation, prayerful reading of the Bible, and retreats; with others, the path of community. The journey outward entails courses in schools of Christian living, once described by writer and spiritual director Elizabeth O'Connor as "part of the training ground for participating in the mission of the church."[15]

Ephrata Cloister provided a second model. In 1732, Conrad Beissel and other German Baptists (Dunkers) founded the community in Lancaster County, Pennsylvania. Among its distinctive practices, Ephrata included celibate brothers and sisters as well as married families.

---

14. Dozier, *Confronted by God*, 29.

15. O'Connor, *Journey Inward, Journey Outward*, 101.

Members recovered several early Christians practices, notably, holding all goods in common as described in Acts 2:43–47 and Acts 4:32–37, and the love feast as described in John 13. The ritual involved footwashing, the Eucharist, and a common meal.

Community members became known for their music, calligraphy, and printing. Following the death of the last celibate member in 1813, the married congregation formed the German Seventh-Day Baptist Church. Members continued to live and worship at the Cloister until 1934. In 1941, the Commonwealth of Pennsylvania acquired the historic site and began a program of restoration. Now a national historical landmark, the grounds are available to a Seventh Day German Baptist congregation that observes the love feast and other rituals.

Apple Farm Community in Three Rivers, Michigan, was a third influence on Brother Graeme. Helen M. Luke (1905–1995) established the center for people seeking to discover the transforming powers of myth and symbol in their lives. Her quiet wisdom drew many people there to reconnect their daily lives with myth and symbol, especially by study of Dante's *Divine Comedy* and Carl Jung's psychology. Brother Graeme encountered a profoundly moving and thrilling truth that the Holy Spirit was moving to free people from existing structures and rules. He began to claim what she described as living imagery arising from the unconscious poet in every person. "The wind blows where it chooses, and you hear the sound of it, but you do not know where it comes from or where it goes. So it is with everyone who is born of the Spirit" (John 3:8).[16]   Brother Graeme visited another community nearby, St. Gregory's, a monastery of men living under the *RB* within the Episcopal church. He also had an opportunity to audit lectures, including a course taught by Henri Nouwen at Yale Divinity School.

In late 1975, Brother Graeme returned to Australia to accept a term-limited position as Associate Pastor at Norlane Baptist Church. Located in an economically depressed, drug-ridden suburb of Geelong, the Norlane congregation had granted a three-year leave of absence to its senior minister, Geoffrey Hunter Malins (1916–2000). Brother Graeme's contract overlapped with Malins' term as a missionary in Papua New Guinea.

---

16. Luke, *Vow and Doctrine in the Age of the Spirit*, 40. For background, Luke, *Dark Wood to White Rose*; Luke, *Autobiography and Journals of Helen M. Luke*.

During his ministry at Norlane, Brother Graeme modeled a balanced life of action and prayer. He met founding members of the Community of the Transformation who were in the youth program: Brothers Os and Neil and Sister Diane. Reaching out to marginalized people, notably women with alcoholic husbands and single mothers who worked as prostitutes to provide their children with school uniforms or meet other essential needs, the embryo Community of the Transfiguration organized cells in three local brothels for needs-based Bible study and family-life programs. They assisted the women to re-train. Many went into teaching, factory work, or other careers. Finally, two of the three brothels closed.

A key program was For Love of Children, or F.L.O.C. Modeled on a Church of the Saviour mission group,[17] F.L.O.C. organized children's activities like school-break outings, birthday parties, and Christmas celebrations. F.L.O.C. grew from twenty-two to over four hundred children within less than six months.

Seeking God more intentionally, a little group in the larger congregation began to listen to the Word of God, the practice of *lectio divina*, which for them entailed not merely reading Scripture, but also meditating on the passages, word for word, phrase by phrase. They paid attention to the promptings of the Spirit and waited for the presence of God to occupy their lives and bring them into union with the Holy One. Their day opened with a prayer of committal and confession followed by a Bible reading, silent reflection, and a brief benediction.

The small group wanted a more communal life of prayer. Some considered celibacy as a lifestyle. One day, Brothers Graeme, Os, and Neil and Sister Diane, swimming in the Moorabool River near Meredith, discussed how, amidst a culture of materialism, they might model the church as reflecting the life of the Holy Trinity. Confused by the absence of support from most Baptist peers and frightened by the risks that lie ahead if they attempted a radical way of life, Brother Os urged, "Let's give it a go and see what happens." They did and, thirty years later, the core group remains together: Brothers Graeme, Os, Neil, and Steve and Sister Diane.

By some measures, Brother Graeme accomplished a great deal during his tenure at Norlane. During the three years, the worshiping con-

---

17. O'Connor, *Journey Inward, Journey Outward*, ch. 10; Cosby, *Handbook for Mission Groups*, 169–70.

gregation grew from sixty to over two hundred and fifty in the morning, and over one hundred and sixty in the evening. Young people formed a fourteen-piece orchestra and forty-member choir. A seed of the future Community of the Transfiguration had begun to germinate.

But everything was not going well. Some Norlane members grumbled about the direction of the work and refused to support it. For example, F.L.O.C.'s annual budget was ten thousand Australian dollars, but not a penny came from the church. There were two main concerns. One was an alleged indifference to Baptist distinctives or lack of accountability to Baptist structures. Another anxiety was a perceived influence of the Charismatic Movement.

Responding to such complaints, Malins returned prematurely to Australia to reclaim control of the congregation. Wounded by this interference, Brother Graeme sought spiritual direction. A relative then serving in Melbourne, the Reverend Richard Littleton, and Val Berg, a spiritual director (mentioned as the Australian Elizabeth O'Connor), helped steady Brother Graeme and the emerging Community of the Transfiguration. Tragically, Val Berg died shortly thereafter with her husband and son. A boat they were in ran aground at sea. A daughter swam to shore, but rescuers arrived too late to save the rest of the family members.

Did the concerns that led to Brother Graeme's premature departure from Norlane have any basis? Interviews and archives reveal that Brother Graeme scrupulously consulted with the Baptist Union of Victoria and with Malins, once flying to New Guinea for dialogue. Also, neither Brother Graeme nor the nascent Community of the Transfiguration was culturally or experientially un-Baptist. They remained loyal to Baptist emphases. Only years later did one member whose religious upbringing was in a Pentecostal congregation join the Community.

As Brother Graeme wound down his ministry at Norlane, he helped to find church homes for those displaced from Norlane. Some people found their way to local Roman Catholic, Anglican, Uniting Church, and Salvation Army congregations where they felt safer. St. Paul's Anglican Church at La Trobe Terrace, and, later, All Saint's Anglican Church in

Newtown, provided space for some to continue their practice of meditative prayer.

At the time, the Baptist Union of Victoria planned to merge Breakwater Baptist Church with Fenwick Baptist Church nearby. Envisioning an alternative future for the Breakwater congregation, Pastor Lindsay Robb (1922–1989) invited Brother Graeme to become his unpaid assistant with the goal of forming an intentional community. By his openness to a Baptist monastic spirituality, Robb helped the two groups move forward.

Breakwater Baptist Church

Geelong is situated in the rich pastoral hinterland of the State of Victoria in Australia. Located on the shores of Corio Bay, on the west of Port Phillip Bay, Geelong is Victoria's second largest city in terms of geography and population. Two hundred and ten thousand persons live in the City of Greater Geelong, increasingly a bedroom community for commuters who make the hour journey by car or train to and from Melbourne each day thanks to infrastructure improvements.

In the mid-nineteenth century, many Christian denominations in the country established congregations to work in Geelong. As early as 1852, the future Aberdeen Street Baptist Church began to meet for Sunday services in a storeroom in a central part of the city.

The suburb where Breakwater Baptist Church is found has an identity of its own. Named for a breakwater constructed with convict labor from 1839–1841 across the Barwon River, the rock ford blocked the inflow of salt water to the river and supplied fresh water to Geelong. In the mid-nineteenth century, Breakwater had an agrarian economy. Chinese residents did market gardening and the Australian Tannery, owned by the Brearley brothers, processed animal goods.[18]

In 1866, members of the Aberdeen Street congregation rented a cottage in the Breakwater neighborhood for a Sunday school. In 1868, the Brearley brothers donated half an acre of land on which to erect a permanent building. Members constructed a plain, rectangular, neo-Georgian-style hall from bluestone, a variety of basalt. With the opening of the

---

18. Roberts, *Cultural Heritage*, 7; photographs also available at http://www.pictureaustralia.org/apps/pictureaustralia.

Sunday school in 1869, Baptists became the first Christian denomination to launch a ministry at Breakwater.

Over the next 135 years, members renovated the building several times, most recently in the early 1990s. On March 27, 1994, Breakwater Baptist Church marked its 125th anniversary. The Palm Sunday service included re-dedication of the original building, now used primarily as a baptistery modeled on a fourth-century one at Ephesus. Another at Tewkesbury Baptist Church in England, dating to the early 1600s, inspired the central position.[19]

A managing committee from the Aberdeen Street Church oversaw the ministry at Breakwater. For ten years, a member named Langhorne walked from downtown Geelong to Breakwater. When no longer physically able to make the journey, he resigned. To ensure continuation of services, members provided transportation. In 1886, when the Breakwater Sunday school marked its first twenty years, the building was free of debt. To accommodate infants the congregation built an addition.

During the next sixty-five years, Baptist work at Breakwater waxed and waned. In World War I, the Young Men's Christian Association used the facility. From 1918 to 1924, Anglicans leased the building at a nominal fee. In April 1924, with help from the Victorian Baptist Home Mission Committee, Baptist witness at Breakwater resumed, continued until 1944, and then suspended.

After World War II, the number of families in Breakwater grew. As a result, in January 1950, the Reverend E. A. Watson, Mr. Graham Lyons, and a group of young people from the Aberdeen Street congregation re-started the Baptist Sunday school at Breakwater.[20] Twenty-five children enrolled. May 7, 1950, saw the resumption of services of worship, initially on the first Sunday afternoon of each month. In 1951, members undertook weekly services and began a mid-week youth club. By 1959, the congregation sought funds for sewerage and building a new room. Ten years later, the congregation celebrated its centenary by opening a modern entrance hall.[21]

From 1965 to 1974, Ern Green, a lay person from Norlane, helped organize weekly services and maintain a youth program. By the 1970s,

19. *Victorian Baptist Witness*, May 1994.

20. *Victorian Baptist Witness*, January 5, 1950.

21. *Bellarine Peninsula Echo*, May 15, 1969.

Breakwater had become a working-class neighborhood with modest housing, factories, and a racecourse. "It was a tough neighborhood then!" commented Deaconess Nola Davies in 1994 at the re-opening of the restored, original bluestone church.[22]

Nola Davies was a key leader from 1972 until 1987, when she took up a position with a Baptist congregation in Geelong East. In the early 1950s, she attended the Victorian Baptist Training Institute, a school that trained women for home or overseas service. Ordained a deaconess in 1959, she worked at Beechworth Baptist and Brunswick Baptist in the early 1960s. Having grown up in Geelong East, she enquired about Breakwater. Baptist Union superintendent J. C. Thompson responded, "Breakwater is not an easy work."[23] She undertook more training after which the home mission committee appointed her to Breakwater Baptist Church.

In 1974, the Reverend Lindsay Robb became the first resident pastor of Breakwater Baptist Church. To house their pastor, his wife Billy, and their children, the congregation purchased a bluestone home contiguous to the original church building. The structure dates to 1846. As dictated by Community needs, HTM has re-modeled it in the 1990s.

Robb served the congregation from 1974 to 1985. On Sunday March 21, 1976, the Baptist Union of Victoria formally constituted eight members and nineteen associates of the Breakwater Baptist Church. Mr. C. P. R. Kitchen, President of the Baptist Union of Victoria, and the administrator responsible for church extension, the Reverend Milton Warn, led the service.[24]

A JOINT JOURNEY

The faithful at Breakwater Baptist had been praying that God would bring new life at Breakwater. Their prayer was answered in a surprising way. When Robb invited the budding Community of the Transfiguration to make Breakwater their home, he proposed that the group use the entrance hall of the bluestone church for compline and an hour of silence

---

22. Nola Davies, "Opening of Restored Church Building, 27/3/94."

23. Letter of June 30, 1960 in the personnel files of Nola Davies, archives of the Baptist Union of Victoria.

24. *Victorian Baptist Witness*, May 5, 1976.

every day. Persons in the group were Brothers Neil, Graeme, Os, and Sister Diane, joined by Carol Bolton and Derek Hooper.

From November 1976 on, each Monday morning the tiny group organized their allotted space with icons, candles, or other furnishings. Each Sunday, the space became more recognizably Baptist. The group wrote new liturgies for baptism, Eucharist, and other celebrations. They developed new rituals, for example, footwashing, or using milk and honey at Easter when Baptismal life is renewed. Some in the Breakwater congregation were unfamiliar with these forms of devotion. After a couple of years, they came to trust and support the Community as a mission group within the local congregation.[25]

The emerging community continued a ministry begun through Norlane Baptist Church. Carol Bolton provided leadership as F.L.O.C. flourished and later came under direction of Geelong City Council. In 1978, a church report called on members to "[p]ray that our love for Jesus will bring all of our children and their mums and dads into the joys that we have because of this blessed Jesus. Pray with us for a bus and a house, and clarity of sight in the way we are to grow."[26] Bolton married a Baptist minister. Hooper moved on to explore other possibilities for his life. Both have remained in touch with the Community.

Outside accountability was important for the group. They turned to the Baptist Union of Victoria for help in discernment. Superintendent Tony Cupit suggested Athol Gill of Whitley College and the House of the Gentle Bunyip. Dr. Robin, Anglican priest at St. Paul's Church in Geelong and Roy Bradley, counselor and founder of clinical pastoral education at the Austin Hospital in Melbourne, also provided supervision. After a year, the group proposed living in two homes near the church for celibate men and celibate women. Their advisors suggested they were not yet ready. After six months, four men moved into one house and two women into another.

From 1977 to 1989, with some overlap of membership, Breakwater Baptist Church and the Community of the Transfiguration existed side by side. In interviews, members recalled their experience of church dur-

---

25. Peter Hobbs and Louise Hobbs, interview by Paul Dekar, July 2, 2004; Don Walker and Jeannette Walker, interview by Paul Dekar, July 24, 2004. The Hobbs and Walkers are members of the Greater Community.

26. Breakwater Baptist Family Church, Annual Report, 1978.

ing those years as a time of "no longer," but "not yet."[27] It was a liminal period during which the ritual subject or person passes through a time betwixt and between. Anthropologist Victor W. Turner has likened liminality to being in the womb, invisibility, darkness, the wilderness, death, or an eclipse of the sun or moon.[28]

Breakwater Baptist Church experienced disintegration and reintegration. Literally, the Community of the Transfiguration moved from the margins, or threshold, to something new, at least in Baptist ecclesiology. During this period, even the architectural setting was liminal. Six days a week, the entrance hall of the bluestone church housed various furnishings that had to be removed for the more traditional Sunday worship of the congregation.

During the 1980s, three key developments took place. One was spiritual and numerical growth. Congregation and Community members deepened their understanding of monastic spirituality and their shared practices. Thirty-six baptisms took place. On September 22, 1982, the annual meeting of Breakwater Baptist Church decided to admit into membership Christians of other denominations who had not necessarily been baptized by immersion as adults.

A second development was the renovation of existing buildings and the construction of two additions to the Cloister. The first major project involved space for the daily offices, periods of prayer in monasteries. Designed and built by Louis Williams, a chapel sat in open fields at Bittern, near Hastings on Western Port, east of Port Phillip Bay. Opened in 1920 by the First Anglican Archbishop of Melbourne, the Most Reverend Henry Lowther Clark, the chapel was then known as St. Martin's. It was to have become part of a much larger complex that, along with a grammar school, would serve the entire district. But the population did not grow as anticipated. For some years, the chapel housed services but later fell into disuse, was vandalized, and closed.

In the early 1970s, Brother Graeme was traveling through the area with Alan E. Lewis, an Anglican priest who was briefly part of the Community. Brother Graeme spotted the abandoned building and squeezed through one of the broken windows. "On that day the Lord promised that He would give it to us."

27. Graeme Littleton, Steve Shipman, and Miriam Toska, interview by Paul Dekar, July 3, 2004.

28. Turner, *Ritual Process*, 94; Chittister, *Fire in These Ashes*; Fisher, "Liminality (I)" and "Liminality (II)."

Passing by the deserted building again in 1979, Brother Graeme recalled the earlier visit and negotiated removal of the building, brick by brick. He found a mould to make additional bricks needed for the

Brother Graeme leading prayer in Oratory

Procession into Oratory

Morning light in Oratory

chapel. A Geelong businessman supplied the red carpet as an expression of gratitude to the Community after his daughter had seen a Community member for counseling.

Consecration of the furnishings, vessels, broadloom, and linens took place on December 3, 1981, followed two days later by the opening of the Oratory. Brother Graeme observed, "It stands . . . a miraculous sign of the extravagance of our God in loving His trusting children."[29]

The next building project began in 1984. Using salvaged bluestone, Peter Hobbs, Don Walker, and other members of the Breakwater congregation built a new toilet block at the rear of the original 1869 church building. They then launched construction of a complex with a library, kitchen, and open space for worship, meetings, teaching, meals, or other gatherings. The project required nine years. Apart from the wiring, Community and parish members did all the other work. They named the hall Ephrata, after the early Baptist community and Bethlehem in the Holy Land, as identified by Gen 35:19. The service of dedication took place in 1993. Thanks to significant support from Fred and Tess Wilby, parents of Sister Terri, and from members of the Greater Community, the project was completed free of debt.

The third major development during the 1980s was the formal establishment of the Community of the Transfiguration as a part of Breakwater

29. Helen Longmuir, a member of the Community of the Transfiguration, has written an illustrated story of the Oratory (August 1985).

Baptist Church. For years under the Victorian Baptist Home Mission Society, a Committee of Management had run the church. On August 4, 1976, at its first annual meeting as a newly constituted congregation, Breakwater Baptist Church formed a deaconate following guidelines of the Baptist Union of Victoria.

As the Holy Transfiguration Monastery began to evolve after 1977, members developed a statement in which they articulated key practices by which they lived. Rather than writing an extensive, potentially rigid rule, they summarized their commitments as follows:

> Jesus calls us to an immediate reconciliation. "Do not let the sun go down on your anger."
>
> While it is today, go to the one you are wounding or who is wounding you and be reconciled; forgive with love or seek forgiveness with humility.
>
> To refuse is to become a stumbling block.
>
> Be courageously resistant towards stubbornness and pride:
>
> consider the grief it brings to Jesus and your brothers and sisters;
>
> Let the Holy Spirit have her way in your heart. Only then will you have peace and bring peace to others. Let love be victorious. Then the kingdom of heaven will dawn in our midst.

For the transition from Norlane to Breakwater, this simple covenant served HTM well. The ideas expressed have remained basic for the Community. Meanwhile, new members were joining the original core group. In 1985, Pastor Robb retired and was succeeded by the Reverend Richard Littleton, who served for three years. Brother Graeme held the title "Prior" of the Community of the Transfiguration. At its annual meeting in October 1987, Breakwater Baptist Church voted to disband the deaconate and to assign responsibility for the life of the congregation to all who made it a spiritual home. Breakwater Baptist Church members agreed to draw together materials that would become the basis of a new constitution.

For fourteen months, little progress was made in terms of integrating the work. Then, in late 1988, a number of persons set about more intentionally to bring the two groups together. Already a great deal had been accomplished towards the intertwining and interdependence of Breakwater Baptist Church and the Community of the Transfiguration.

Church folk and members of the Community of the Transfiguration all gave input on a mechanism to draw up new structures. At a church meeting on January 15, 1989, members agreed to the process. Over the next two months, each person wrote statements as to where he/she saw the congregation and Community going. A joint committee collected documents and ideas under these headings:

1. Beliefs: God, Salvation, Scriptures, Repentance, Prayer, Transfiguration

2. The Church: Nature and ministry of the Church, Sacraments of the Church (Baptism and Eucharist); Present Direction of Breakwater Church; Spirituality, and Mission

3. Canon: Name, Basis of Fellowship, Membership, Offices, Meetings, Finances, Property, Order, and Discipline

For the next six months, the new constitution went through various drafts. On November 26, 1989, church and Community accepted the constitution for ten years. Peter Hobbs wrote,

> Our constitution, which was a combined effort of many of us here at Breakwater, has given us a certain sense of security. It helps us when we endeavour to explain our unique life here. The constitution has been given to a number of other pastors and to members of the Baptist Union, and the comments from these people have been very favourable.[30]

The new constitution paved the way for integration of the Community of the Transfiguration and Breakwater Baptist Church. In effect, all members of Breakwater Baptist became part of the Community of the Transfiguration, living either in the Cloister or nearby. Non-Baptists kept their membership in their respective denominations. On March 27, 1994, a service marked the 125th anniversary of Breakwater Baptist Church. Members looked back at its pilgrimage. Like that of most congregations, it was filled with great joy and great pain, a small but sincere effort that, "joined with God's grace will continue to fulfill our ancient destiny in sometimes colourful and surprising ways."[31]

30. Peter Hobbs (secretary), "Breakwater Baptist Church, the Making of Our Constitution" (August 1991), 3.

31. Bulletin, 125th Anniversary of Breakwater Baptist Church.

In addition to developing an extensive, forty-seven page constitution, members have worked hard to clarify the shared vision of Community and Congregation. An eighty-eight page document called *Testament and Pastoral Rule* explores the theology and practices of the Community. A seventy-nine page collection of stories, sayings, and statements called *The Beacons* has proved influential and directive in the Community's life. John Blomfield of Drysdale, a short drive east of Geelong, contributed the illustrations.

In the mid-1990s, Community members began revising their covenant. Members read and reflected on drafts during the Offices and in silent prayer. Community members agreed to a text known as the Resolve. They placed it on a large banner hung in the main hall and printed copies as a flyer that they could display in their homes. The fruit of experience over a thirty-year period, the Resolve is neither a legal nor a static document. Shaping the identity and common life of members, it has been and may again be revised. We return to the Resolve in chapter 4. For now, it is sufficient simply to present the text as it reads in 2007:

> Being perfectly assured of your salvation,
> with your whole life proclaim your gratitude.
> Reject nothing, consecrate everything.
> Be the good of love, for God, for neighbor, for all creation.
> Judge no one, not even yourself.
> Love beauty.
> Maintain inner-silence in all things.
> Show hospitality; err only on the side of generosity.
> Speak truth to power, especially power without love.
> Let your only experience of evil be in suffering, not its creation.
> For us there is only the trying, the rest is none of our business.

In 2001, a revised constitution adopted the name Holy Transfiguration Community and identified several ways by which members could identify with the Community: those living in the Cloister under a common purse in accord with Acts 2:45 and Acts 4:34; members of the Greater Community that regularly tithe and share at the Cloister; members of Sketes; and Companions to the Community, and those in covenant with the Community.[32]

---

32. HTM, "Baptist Church in Breakwater, 1869–2001," 27.

At the time of writing, there are two houses of prayer, the Cloister in Breakwater and St. Luke's in Melbourne. Members of the Greater Community include those living near these two centers and those at a greater distance who are exploring ways to strengthen their relationship with the Community. To describe the Community of the Transfiguration, members call it a community of autonomous houses of prayer committed to monastic spirituality, united by the Resolve and a weekly rhythmic celebration of the life of Jesus, Word Made Flesh, intentionally communal, primarily contemplative, and inclusive in theological focus and practice. From a deepening, transfiguring, life-preserving experience of the love of God, members reach out to the world, owning the humbling, safeguarding frustration of a localized, limited ability to respond.[33]

By 2006, Community members faced two problems. First, the Breakwater Cloister was running out of space to accommodate those seeking to join the novitiate or explore monastic life. Second, the populace around the City of Greater Geelong was expected to grow by over a hundred thousand in the next few years. To serve commuters to Melbourne, a new railroad station has opened near the monastery. This has resulted in an increase of invasive noise. As well, the State of Victoria has planned to build a major arterial road for industrial traffic near the monastery. The project will run within a hundred yards of the monastery's present location.

With a clear sense of their vocation to witness to the one true God and with determination to deal creatively with these problems, members weighed options including the possibility of re-locating. Consulting Baptist Union of Victoria leaders at every step, members began to look for appropriate land.

As of August 2007, the Community has secured eighteen acres of land twenty-five miles away at Teesdale, just off the Midland Highway from Geelong to Ballarat, and has accepted a contract for the sale of the church property, to be followed before the end of the year by sale of four homes occupied by Community members. It has submitted plans to appropriate authorities for construction of fourteen homes and other buildings at Teesdale. It has arranged temporary accommodations for members during the transition. To cover start-up costs, the Community has received several grants, including one from the State of Victoria to

33. HTM, "Holy Transfiguration Community," 2005.

ensure ecologically sound development of water supplies at the new Cloister.

The Community plans to leave Breakwater by the end of January 2008. A further step in the journey is about to unfold.

REFLECTIONS ON THE COMMUNITY'S HISTORY

For thirty-five years, the Community of the Transfiguration has moved from one way of being the local church to another: from congregation to Community, and from Community to monastery. From this survey of the Community's history, three features stand out. First, HTM is a Baptist monastery. By virtue of its Baptist identity, HTM differs from the overwhelming majority of monasteries, intentional communities, and centers of renewal. By virtue of its monastic identity, HTM differs fundamentally from most Baptist congregations.

Second, HTM exhibits many generic traits of its monastic forebears and of the new monastic communities. These include the centrality of Jesus Christ, communal life under a rule of life, vital worship, use of the visual arts, care for youth, care for the natural world; and ministries among marginalized persons. In this sense, the life of Community members is neither unique, nor original, perhaps only "newly born . . . a spirit and an endless trying, changing and beginning again."[34]

Third, HTM has been stable for a generation and is already looking to a future beyond the life span of the founders. HTM members have been on a journey similar to that of the new monastics in North America. With creativity, faithfulness, integrity, and love, members have experience a deepened knowledge of God, whose love is greater than any evil and has triumphed not only over evil, but also over self. This aspect of their journey has real significance for Community members and for those whose lives they have touched. People who are used to being rejected and abandoned have found acceptance and unconditional love at the Community.

In a letter dated July 19, 2006, and addressed to the Reverend Alan Marr, Director of Ministries, and the Executive Council of the Baptist Union of Victoria, Community members reflected on their calling and growing monastic spirituality. They characterized the monastery as

---

34. HTM, "Testament and Pastoral Rule," 87.

a sacred site, a holy place, a concentration of Presence, generosity, and love, in a non-judgmental environment. For pilgrims it is a refuge—a safe place to rest for a while, to ask life's questions and to receive "knowing" without "understanding." It is an anchorage for the soul, always open for you—a place to ultimately belong, to anchor yourself to, even if you only visit once in a while. A well spring, known to you, somewhere you can go, an actual place—a focus of deep, abiding, healing, fertile stillness—an outpost of the Kingdom of God.

As the monastery prepares to move to Teesdale, the Baptist Union of Victoria has officially accepted HTM as a Monastery of the denomination. This experience has been mutually powerful and freeing. Rather than being marginalized, members of the Community of the Transfiguration have claimed their identity as God's beloved. To quote the Reverend Dr. Frank Rees, principal of Whitley College of the Melbourne College of Divinity since 2006, the Community is "permission-giving. When we come, we are free simply to be ourselves."

On August 4, 2007, a service at the Breakwater Cloister recognized this and celebrated the Feast of the Transfiguration. One expression of how to be Baptist, HTM is not in competition with, nor does it deny the right of any other congregation to express Baptist identity in another way. That the Baptist Union of Victoria embraces HTM with all its diversity is a positive affirmation of the radical love and witness extended by Community members to so many people.

In contemporary terms, HTM members "walk the talk." Their action in the world comes from obedience understood as both a communal and a personal listening to the voice of God. HTM members do not perceive their life as a burden or sacrifice. Praying to be conscious, honest, simple, and merciful, members offer a radical way in the building and restoring of loving relationships with God, self, others, and all creation. They are asked only to try—not to succeed—to live holy lives. Their life in God has brought them great fulfillment, personally and in Community, and opened up paths of servanthood in areas of great need.

In chapter 3, we examine the practices of HTM members. In chapter 4, we examine the theology of the Resolve.

THREE

Practices of Holy Transfiguration Monastery

INTRODUCTION

While the cultural context of HTM is quite different than that of the new monastic communities in the United States and elsewhere, each of the marks of the new monasticism mentioned earlier are evident at HTM. In this chapter, we highlight several of the practices manifest in the lives of HTM members. In chapter 4, we explore the theological foundations for these and other practices. A notice board and words outside the Cloister in Breakwater introduce key practices:

> Here some of the People of GOD from many Christian Communions live together as an intentional Monastic Community. In an age of growing fear and terrorism, we search for peace and unity in a profound union with GOD. We have found it is the human heart that must first be disarmed. We strive to pray our life and to live our prayer, to be conscious, honest, simple and merciful towards all people and the earth. Here the "Prayer of the Heart"—of compassion and gratitude—has not failed. We share our life with any in need.

PRACTICES OF THE CHURCH

HTM describes itself as an intentional monastic community. As well, it is a Baptist congregation of the Baptist Union of Victoria. How intentionally Baptist is HTM? As successors of the sixteenth-century continental Anabaptists, the seventeenth-century Puritans, and the eighteenth-century Brethren, Baptists around the world share a legacy that has inspired democracy and the championing of religious freedom, promoting justice through struggles for the abolition of slavery, against colonialism, for women's rights or for human rights.

HTM recognizes its Baptist identity in many ways. It emphasizes such distinctive aspects of Baptist polity as separation of church and state, commitment to the teachings of the Bible, the importance of a personal knowledge of God and relationship with Christ, the priesthood of all believers, the centrality of the sacraments of Baptism and Eucharist, and congregational polity. It is a member of the Baptist Union of Victoria. It pays its full share of fees per member to the denomination. Three successive superintendents of the Baptist Union of Victoria have served as advisors. Members attend Baptist Union of Victoria gatherings, occasionally as leaders of workshops. Every month, Baptist Union of Victoria leaders spend a quiet day at HTM, as do several Baptist pastors.

The denomination holds title to the Community's property. At its own expense and effort, the Community of the Transfiguration has quadrupled the value of the original Breakwater Baptist Church property. Having acquired four adjoining properties, the Community has transferred these titles to the name of the Baptist Union of Victoria with provisions that protect the interests of both parties. Lawyers have drawn up similar deeds for the Teesdale property. Community members see this as an act of identity and solidarity with the Baptist Union of Victoria and their mutual welfare.

How intentionally ecumenical is HTM? HTM members recognize a unity that transcends denominational particularity. Their ecumenism is relational, not official or structural. Members overcome differences by living in community, praying together, and struggling with the pain of a common humanity. The Community celebrates the Eucharist each Thursday and on other feast days. Each Holy Week, members renew their commitment to live out of their baptism.

The celebration of each of these rituals is a time of giving thanks, in Greek *eucharisteo*, from which the name of the Eucharistic liturgy derives. The liturgies mediate the powerful and experienced reality of Community members that they are one with God, with one another, and with the entire cosmos. The liturgies are not sources of division or exclusion. To quote the *Testament and Pastoral Rule*, it is the praxis of HTM members to share in the sacraments courageously.

> **Baptism.** By baptism we are made "one family" in Christ. By baptism we transcend all political, ethnic, gender, social, sexual, cultural, intellectual, hierarchical, denominational, academic differences.
>
> **Eucharist.** Being many, we are One bread, One body.
> Eucharist is the perpetuation and sustaining of baptismal life.
> We will have an open table, open to all the people of God to preside, participate, and receive.

The Community goes on to refer to a World Council of Churches consultation held in 1994 at Iasi, Romania, on "Christian Spirituality for Our Times." It quotes the final report as follows, "Christian spirituality rooted in the suffering, reconciling, and uniting love of God in the world, is affronted and even astonished by broken bread and poured out wine that cannot be fully shared. It should be understood, then, that a genuine ecumenical commitment to deepen Christian spirituality for our times is likely to further provoke an ecumenical crisis over the unfulfilled expectation of Eucharistic hospitality. And so it should!"[1]

Community of the Transfiguration members seek advice from many sources. They freely make themselves accountable to authorities of all the communions represented in the monastery. They have consulted with representatives of two Anglican (Episcopalian) monasteries: St. Mark's Abbey, a Benedictine monastery in Camperdown, and the Community of the Holy Name in Melbourne. It also has relations with members of Tarrawarra Abbey, a Cistercian monastery located near Yarra Glen in the valley of the Yarra River, and with the Little Brothers of St. Francis, an eremitical community located at Tabulam in northern New South Wales.[2]

For over thirty-five years, members of the Community of the Transfiguration have explored and lived out of traditional monastic spirituality. This has made the Community somewhat of a working model, or

1. HTM, "Testament and Pastoral Rule," 16–17; *Mid-Stream* 33, 4 (October 1994): 473–81 for a text of the report.

2. Michael Casey, OCSO, interview by Paul Dekar, June 18, 2004; Michael King, OSB, interview by Paul Dekar, June 10, 2004; Philippa Pickering, CHN, interview by Paul Dekar, June 23, 2004.

bridge, between past and contemporary forms of monastic religious life. As a result, traditional as well as new monastic communities are seeking out the Community of the Transfiguration.

For example, in March and April 2006, Brothers Graeme, Steve, and Os visited the United Kingdom and the United States. They met with seminarians and with members of several intentional communities.

In October 2006, Brothers Stephen and Neil traveled to a village on the Thai side of the border between Burma (Myanmar) and Thailand. Because of her prior experience with the Karen refugees, the Reverend Ann Lock, HTM Chaplain and pastor of Brunswick Baptist Church in Brunswick, Melbourne, accompanied them. Consultants on a building project, they also offered pastoral care and listened as victims of the corrupt regime in their homeland pleaded, "Do not forget us."

In January 2007, Brothers Steve and Stephen and Sister Anna were in New Zealand for ten days. They participated in several gatherings involving hundreds of people from many groups on aspects of monastic spirituality, sustainability of intentional community, and how to deal with the dark side of one's personal and corporate self.

In mid-2007, Brother Wayne of the Franciscan hermitage in New South Wales and Bishop Graeme Rutherford of the House of Bishops took the initiative to invite HTM to be present as observers at meetings of the Anglican Religious Advisory Board in Australia for the next two years. They felt that HTM needed to experience these meetings to see if they could be of any help to HTM, and vice versa.[3] Such a move to involve a non-Anglican community in what is currently a purely Anglican Religious Advisory Board answerable to the House of Bishops is courageous and fraught with possibilities for future ecumenical and inter-monastic cooperation in Australia and worldwide.

Sister Miriam represents the Uniting Church in a formal dialogue process with the Lutheran Church in Australia. HTM regularly hosts the dialogue team. Without sacrificing their core values, HTM members exchange ideas with visitors and inter-faith delegations from a number of denominations and teaching centers.

As these varied invitations and contexts suggest, HTM members move easily and in an unthreatening way across many boundaries within Christianity and outside it. In ecumenical and inter-faith contexts, they

---

3. Bishop Rutherford, e-mail to Paul Dekar, April 22, 2007.

offer a depth of experience of monastic spirituality, of wisdom in dealing with crises that inevitably erupt in community living, and of sensitivity to varied practices among different communions. They have discovered as true what Jesuit theologian William Johnston described of his experience when Christians and Buddhists came together in Japan. He wrote, "We found that dialogue based on theology and philosophy did not achieve much; but when we talked from experience we suddenly discovered how closely united we really were."[4]

In the past, the Baptist Union of Victoria has often been perceived as anti-ecumenical. HTM has played a crucial role in involving Victorian Baptists in wider ecumenical activities through hospitality, relationship building, living together, and participation in inter-monastic and inter-denominational dialogue. HTM has modeled grass roots ecumenism in non-threatening, practical, and relational ways. One can neither measure nor disparage the breadth, depth, and practical impact of this little group's hospitality.[5]

To offer an example, in 1993 the Reverend Robert W. Gribben, then General Secretary of the Victorian Council of Churches (1989–1995) and now Professor of Worship and Mission at the Melbourne College of Divinity, approached HTM to assist an Ethiopian Orthodox congregation made up largely of immigrants fleeing famine in Ethiopia. This led the community to aid the priest of the church to settle into Melbourne with financial and material assistance. Then, the brothers and sisters renovated the inside of their church so that the congregation could celebrate their liturgies as in Ethiopia. This included building their iconostasis, altar, and lavabo, and securing their sanctuary vestments and curtaining for the celebration of their rites according to their rubrics.

Archbishop Nicodemus came from Addis Ababa, Ethiopia, for the consecration of the new church. He visited Breakwater and gifted the Community of the Transfiguration with an ancient Ethiopian cross. HTM also assisted in uniting Ethiopian families who have been separated

4. Johnson, *Silent Music*, 9.

5. John Simpson, immediate past General Superintendent, Baptist Union of Victoria and pastor in Portland, interview by Paul Dekar, June 21, 2004; Alan Marr, current Director of Ministries, interview by Paul Dekar, June 24, 2004; Mark G. Brett of Whitley College, Melbourne, interview by Paul Dekar, July 16, 2004.

by the refugee crisis. Members of the two congregations continue to pray and worship together.[6]

How intentionally monastic is HTM? HTM members believe that monasticism is a universal gift to the Church. Its spirit has been expressed in nearly all traditions of the Christian faith. To visit HTM is to recognize Orthodox, Catholic, and Protestant influences. However, these have not been intentionally developed, but are organic similarities that have spontaneously emerged as the community searched for the truth that harmonized with the needs of their collective identity.

Mount Athos, near Thessalonika, Greece, is one of the centers of Orthodox monastic spirituality visited by HTM members. In its heyday, the monastic republic numbered forty thousand monks and hermits, but the population fell sharply after World War I. During the 1980s, when I visited, there were signs of renewal. Fueled by a growing questioning of modern society on the part of Greeks, and others shaped by Orthodoxy, and since the 1990s by the collapse of the former Soviet Union, the number of vocations and of visitors has increased dramatically.

HTM members have also visited many Catholic and Anabaptist communities, as well as new experimental intentional communities. HTM members study together and draw on both classic monastic sources and contemporary writers such as James Alison, Dietrich Bonhoeffer, Joan Chittister, Rene Girard, Donald B. Kraybill, Thomas Merton, Evelyn Underhill, Jean Vanier, J. Denny Weaver, Walter Wink, and others. They have found inspiration in Baptist antecedents, including communal forms of the sixteenth-century Anabaptist and eighteenth-century Pietist movements, as well as monastic expressions in contemporary Baptist life in Africa and Europe.

HTM members believe they are called to re-plant and nurture monastic life in the midst of an exploitative, consumer-oriented, individualistic society. By their observance of monastic practices such as obedience and stability and the common purse, they seek to live lives that are congruent with commitments in the Resolve such as gratitude, love, prayer, hospitality, and truth-telling. They seek to manifest "the same mind as was in Christ Jesus" (Phil 2:5). Offering radical love, HTM members challenge the domination and reign of evil, first within their own hearts, and then in the world.

6. *Victorian Baptist Witness*, March 1994; Robert W. Gribben, interview by Paul Dekar, July 1, 2004.

Community during silent meditation in Oratory

THE PRACTICE OF PRAYER

Silence, stillness, and solitude dominate the rhythm of prayer for HTM every day. By "The Prayer of the Heart," HTM refers to the innermost core of the person, the True Self where God indwells. In Orthodoxy, the phrase "prayer of the heart" refers to the Jesus Prayer, "Lord Jesus Christ, Son of God, have mercy on me, a sinner." Traditionally, saying the Jesus Prayer sustains friendship with Jesus and fulfills the injunction of Paul to "pray without ceasing" (1 Thess 5:17). For HTM members, life at the

Cloister does not contain or limit one's practice of monastic living. To pray without ceasing means to pray wherever one finds oneself and to recognize God in that place and in the people there. This can only be sustained by the establishment and maintaining of an "inner silence" and solitude, which is realized "within" through the daily rhythm of personal and communal silence, stillness, and liturgical prayer.

Jesus provided a model for prayer. Jesus began and ended his model prayer (Matt 5:9–13; Luke 11:2–4) by acknowledging the holiness of God. He offered God adoration and prayed that God's realm be established on earth as in heaven. Jesus then petitioned God to nourish, to forgive, to protect from temptation, and to deliver from evil. In a few brief phrases, Jesus was making a crucial point. Prayer did not insulate him from the world. He wanted people to know that, as they responded to the gracious call to follow him, prayer should shape their spirituality for life in the here-and-now, as well as in the realm to come.

The Lord's Prayer includes these words, "Your will be done on earth as it is in heaven." This phrase establishes a crucial connection between one's eternal relationship with Jesus and one's ordinary life in the world. God reigns on earth as in heaven. The prayer of the heart connects the one who prays with concerns in the real world.

Through the prayer of the heart, HTM members open their hearts to the world in which God took flesh and seek to live with loving kindness, justice, and compassion. They cite thoughts of Staretz Silouan (1866–1938), a monk of Mount Athos whose spiritual journey gave him wisdom and insight he imparted to others. Just before he died, he said that monasticism had to come down from the mountain and be in the world because the need of the world was so great.[7]

The first call of the day is to be alone with God. Going to the Oratory during the early hours of the morning, members gather in silence, stillness, and solitude, generally at least fifteen minutes before the Office. Morning Prayer begins at 7:30 a.m. This corporate time of prayer has a simple structure punctuated with silence and the reading of the Scriptures, including the Psalms, intercessions, and the commitment of life and work to the glory of God for the day. The brothers and sisters maintain silence for thirty minutes after the Morning Office and meet briefly around 8:30 to review the work of the day. Those able gather again at the Oratory for

7. Sophrony, *Monk of Mount Athos*, 46–49, 73.

Sister praying before an icon

Sister meditating along cloister walk

Transfiguration of Christ; glass etching

the Midday Office and at 7 p.m. for compline, which is preceded by thirty minutes of corporate silence and stillness. Compline is followed by silence or spiritual reading. At 8:30 p.m., households meet to be with each other and relax. Curfew is at 10 p.m., after which Community members maintain silence until Morning Prayer the next day.

The beauty, simplicity, and holiness of the Cloister, both the buildings, the icons, stained glass, and other artistic features make it possible for members to pray anywhere. The Community has benefited from the gifts of members who are trained as architects, as artists, and in several crafts. Masters in their respective media, they have designed and built or renovated three buildings used for corporate prayer, *lectio divina*, and personal, contemplative prayer.

Many Community members use the Jesus Prayer, the Lord's Prayer, and other set prayers, as well as praying before icons as an aid to prayer. While the use of icons is uncommon in Protestant circles, the practice has served as a point of connection with Christ and the community of saints and thereby enlivened the prayer life of Community members.

Two icons are especially prominent in activity of prayer at HTM. One is the icon of the Holy Trinity by Andrei Rublev. Written for the monastery of the Trinity and St. Sergius between 1408 and 1425, it is now housed in the Tretiakof Gallery in Moscow. The icon depicts the story in Gen 18:1–15, wherein God appeared to Abraham by the oaks of Mamre. Abraham looked up, saw three men standing near him, and asked his wife to prepare food. During the meal, Sarah and Abraham learned that, despite their advanced age, they would have a son.

In interviews with HTM members, I learned that they focus on the icon not for its depiction of the Biblical event, or for its theology of the Trinity. Rather, many Community members are drawn to the icon by its invitation to dwell with joy in the presence of the Holy One who receives everyone in love and forgiveness.

Another Biblical image especially meaningful to many HTM members is that of Christ Pantokrator, the triumphant Christ in whom all things hold together (Col 1:17). One artistic rendering of this idea is found in a mosaic over the central door of the narthex at Hagia Sophia in Istanbul. The scene depicts Pope Leo VI prostrate before Christ enthroned. In a detail crucial for community members, the icon depicts the Lord's left foot as cloven. In this way, the icon portrays the Risen One as holding all opposites together in a creative tension, both the good and the sin of our lives.[8]

There is an ancient Christian tradition holding that, as Jesus entered the waters of baptism, the Jordan River suddenly burst into flames. So was seen the coming together of the opposites that, against their natures, did not cancel each other out. Rather, by the presence of the Creator and Redeemer, they co-existed in a harmony that gave birth to new life in Fire

8. Weitzmann, *Icon*, 25.

and Water, Babylon and Jerusalem, Gentile and Jew, Slave and Free, Male and Female, Good and Evil. In community, HTM members affirm that they owe their existence to the Holy One who is able to hold all opposites in tension so that new life can come.

Members use prayers and liturgies that are informed by ancient traditions. However, the language is contemporary, dynamic, meditative, poetic, and socially attuned. Singing is central, and HTM has again benefited from the gifts of Community members and Companions.

The Community of the Transfiguration follows the Christian year with liturgies unique to Advent, Epiphany, Lent, Easter, Ascension, Pentecost, and Transfiguration (August 6). Since antiquity, the western churches have observed the Transfiguration at the time of Lent. However, HTM follows the tradition by which Anglican and Orthodox communions observe the Feast of the Transfiguration on August 6.[9] HTM marks its origins in 1972 around September 14, Feast Day of the Holy Cross.

Ringing bells at start of daily offices

9. Ouspensky and Lossky, *Meaning of Icons*, 211.

Community members at rehearsal

Community members remove shoes when entering places of worship,
including during Wednesday rehearsals

HTM members meditate on key events in the life of Jesus in a weekly
rhythm. On Mondays, they focus on the incarnation. At noon they con-

nect their lives with the One who embraced pain and redeemed suffering from meaninglessness and despair. The liturgy recalls the uncreated Light who came into the world as "pain-bearer."[10] HTM members believe, but pray for courage in unbelief (Mark 9:24). They know that, "just as the sufferings of Christ are abundant for us, so also our consolation is abundant through Christ . . . and salvation" (2 Cor 1:5–6).

Tuesdays, they recall the baptism of Jesus. In words at noon, members recall that as Jesus descended into the Jordan River and experienced intensely the blessing of the presence of the Holy Spirit, so he descended into the depths of the waters of the unconscious in order to bring liberation, salvation, and redemption to the human psyche. He now speaks in the unconscious of the believer as he was empowered by the divine voice in tones of acceptance and joy.

Wednesdays, members focus on the transfiguration, a *theophany* of divine and human disclosure from which HTM has taken its name. Peter, James, and John were witnesses to the transfiguration (Mark 9:2–8 and parallels; 2 Pet 1:16–21). They came to understand that a new dimension of God's realm had broken in. They were witnesses to the glory of a human being fully alive, the first of their own kind, which the *shekinah* (glory) of God validated and accepted.

At noon on Wednesdays members contemplate an icon of Jesus enveloped by the *shekinah* of God. They reflect on this insight: each person is to come into perpetual union with the Divine. This indeed is the calling of every person. "The light and glory of His flesh and His clothing on the mountain is what happens to any part of creation raised to its fulfillment in union with the Divine. Both the saints and the earth itself have manifested this glory at times in the history of salvation."

Wednesday evenings, the Community's prayers are brief. In preparation for the Thursday liturgy, or any other special liturgies being planned, Community members review the worship and practice the music. Members discuss any issues that have arisen or decisions that need to be made. Sometimes, a Community member or invited guest teaches. Over a number of years, Brother Graeme has lectured on Dante and the *Divine Comedy*, as well as on contemplative prayer, dreams, and other subjects related to the psychological dimensions of the spirituality of the Community. These talks have brought many friends to the Community.

---

10. *Evening Prayer and Testimony for the Season of the Transfiguration of Our Lord.* For this language, HTM members refer to Brueggemann, "Gospel Language of Pain and Possibility" and "Shape for Old Testament Theology, II: Embrace of Pain."

Entry into Oratory

These lectures are not weekly. Wednesday evenings are generally kept as a midweek Sabbath. Members are free to do whatever they wish they can: visit relatives or friends, play sport, relax with each other, enjoy a meal in town, and so on. All return home by 9:00 p.m.

As HTM members reflected on the rhythm of Jesus' life and relevant passages in the Bible, they came to a more sacramental understanding of the Eucharist, specifically, and more generally of the way by which God uses ordinary things like water, bread, and wine to mediate the presence and mystery of God's saving action. They also searched out and activated ethical implications in their lives of their baptism and of Jesus'

Eucharist. The 1999 constitution emphasized the transformative nature of Eucharistic and baptismal ethics.

> Anyone anticipating membership in this Community needs to be resolved and committed to the transfiguration of their person. This will involve the legitimate anguish of accountability and the joy and exhilaration of new discovery . . . nothing short of a transformation *of this* life—politically, economically, socially and spiritually—and *in this* life, of heart, mind and being (Ezek 36:26–28). In Baptism and through perpetual Eucharistic Celebration we engage in a life-long process of transfiguration into the life of Christ (Rom 12:1–2), "being conformed to His likeness from one degree of glory to another" (2 Cor 3:18).[11]

Thursdays, HTM celebrates the Eucharist in words appropriate to the liturgical cycle and "with joyful urgency in the belief that life can be radically different." Emphasis is very clearly on the cost of a new beginning, confession, forgiveness, and the cancellation of every debt. Having set early Christian prayers to contemporary language, Community members express both their experience of absolution of sin, and their determination to live in the light of the love of God.

I first visited the Community in July 1998. In one of their prayers, Community members had adapted words of St. Basil the Great. As HTM continued to reflect on the ethical dimension of participating in Eucharist, in 2006 it expanded the prayer that read as follows:

> *Cantor:* The bread which we do not use
>
> *All:* is the bread of the hungry.
>
> *C:* The garment hanging in our wardrobe
>
> *A:* is the garment of one who is naked.
>
> *C:* The shoes that we do not wear
>
> *A:* are the shoes of one who is barefooted.
>
> *C:* The money we keep locked away
>
> *A:* is the money of the poor.
>
> *C:* The acts of charity we do not perform
>
> *A:* are the many injustices we commit.

---

11. HTM, "Testament and Pastoral Rule," 14–15, emphasis in original.

A: Lord, I am no longer my own but Yours. Put me to what You will. Put me to doing. Put me to being. Put me to suffering. Let me be employed for You—or laid aside for You. Let me be full—let me be empty. Let me have all things—let me have nothing. Help me to open my eyes when others close theirs; to hear when others don't wish to listen; to look when others turn away; to seek to understand when others give up; to rouse myself when others acquiesce; to continue to struggle even when I am not the strongest; to cry out when others are silent; to be Christians in Community. First of all that, then further, to live when others are dead and Be Love when society is too mean and self-obsessed to remember. We love You Lord and so give ourselves. Amen.

In 2006, the Thursday Eucharist concluded with a commission and blessings: "Go out into the world. Make it your first work to Love others. Say that the Kingdom of Heaven has come. The Lord says, Walk before my face and be whole. My Presence shall go with you and I will give you rest. Behold I am with you every moment even to the end of the world." As is generally the case, the celebration continued in a substantial meal shared with everyone present whether or not he or she had attended the Eucharistic liturgy.

On Friday mornings the Community contemplates the crucifixion of Jesus. At noon each Friday, the Community reflects on the darkness that murders the Word made flesh, the Creator and Sustainer of all things with these words:

O Creator of all, today You are struck down by Your creation.

When You were transfigured on the mountain, O Lord,

Your disciples saw the glory of the first of their own kind.

And when they saw You crucified,

they knew that Your suffering and death were voluntary,

and would then proclaim to the ages to come

that You are truly the "New Creation."

Cantor: Lord I stand before You.

All: You have taken my hand.

C: You will lead me by Your counsel.

A: And bring me home to Your glory.

C: Let us say with all our mind and with all our heart:

A: Glory be to Thee O Lord, Glory be to Thee.

Baskets for washday

Friday evening, the Community contemplates the burial of Jesus the Savior, which includes silent intercessions for the world. After the Office, Community members enjoy an evening together. It may simply mean eating together and watching a movie for entertainment, for example, one featuring Charlie Chaplain or from the Catherine Cookson collection. Often, retreatants and Companions who live at or near the Cloister join in the informal gathering.

Saturday mornings provide opportunities to care for the grounds, to rest, and to prepare other offices. There is no corporate Morning Prayer. At noon, the Community celebrates the descent of the Holy One into the realm of the dead. A meditative reflection at the beginning of the Midday Office is as follows:

> Yesterday we watched our Saviour and True God die. Today we celebrate God's disappearance from the earth and Christ's presence in Hell. Hell is the place of a terrifying vulnerability and helplessness, the place where all that "liminality" is, is experienced. That place of "no longer" and "not yet." The land of the Dead is the realm of the unresolved—the unanswered—the place of the unredeemed—it is that time in Baptismal life when what is valued and essential for Life sinks to an unknown place and takes us with it.

In You we meet the Immortal One who wounds and heals, who casts down and raises up, who makes small and makes large. The One who gives life and takes it away, the One in whom all opposites find their meeting place. In a word the One who makes us whole. The very enormity of such an experience gives it its value and magnifies its shattering impact. Sublime—pregnant with meaning—yet chilling our blood and paralyzing our very desire to live, it rises out of the Mystery we were baptized into (Death, Burial, and Resurrection) and embraces us in a love so strong that we no longer have any control. While such an experience never exceeds the bounds of human capacities, it does rend from top to bottom the curtain that protects us in our ordered "outside" worlds from a direct personal encounter with the Divine Other—God the wondrous Mystery of Love. Until that curtain at the entrance of the soul is penetrated and rent in two, we shall never know the life that rises out of the unfathomable abyss of the unborn, or see things that eyes have not seen and hear things which ears have not heard, nor experience what the heart cannot conceive. Because the earthly pilgrimage of every baptized person is modeled on the Life of Christ, is it any wonder that as He was crucified in His day, so we experience the crucifixion of the Church in our own. Surely the 20th century is the Holy Saturday of history—the time of God's death and disappearance from life. For the whole world and the Church and in particular each of the Baptized I believe it is so. "The earthly fate of the Church as the Body of Christ is modeled on the earthly fate of Christ Himself. That is to say the Church in the course of her history moves towards a death . . . until at last her Lord, after fulfilling her task, she dies in failure and disappears."[12]

The Collect that closes the Midday Office speaks of the Presence of the Holy One in Hell, covered in wounds yet undiminished in forgiving love and compassion, is as follows:

O Christ our Hope, You left the Cross of anguish and entered at the lowest door into the realm of the dead. Into the sorrowful labyrinth of darkness You cast the Light of transfigured humanity. The despairing awoke to a fresh and lively smell of mercy and love. You became their peace and only light—the prophetic dew—proclaiming the dawn of joy in a new beginning. On your breast, O

12. Hugo Rahner, quoted in Jung, *Mysterium Conjunctionis*, vol. 14 of *Collected Works*, para. 28, n. 194.

Lord, they laid their grief and shame, and with You eagerly left their captivity for ever. O Jesus our true God and Saviour, remember us this day in Your Kingdom.

After 6:00 p.m. on Saturday evening, the Community celebrates the resurrection of Jesus and the hope of their own salvation. The evening liturgy is the beginning of the Christian Sabbath for the Community—the same one that their Muslim friends nearby celebrated on Friday and that the Jewish friends of the Community celebrated on Saturday. The liturgy announces a day of rest in celebration of the resurrection of Jesus. Literally, Community members experience it as an unstructured, free day for being with each other as in God's realm. The day is not only a day set apart but more so a disposition, a rest in the human heart when God rests in the life of believers and they in turn rest in God.

The Sabbath liturgy opens with words of welcome: "Blessed be God who gives us the Sabbath and leads us to the waters of stillness." God's people reply: "Who restores our soul and commands us to rest." The liturgist says, "Welcome this day. Receive the gift. Remember the Sabbath and keep it. It is made for you, your freedom, your joy, your healing."

During the service, a rich, fruit-filled celebratory Sabbath loaf of bread is blessed and broken. The liturgist holds it up and calls out, "The bread of sincerity and truth." Congregants respond, "The joy and pain of our life." The large loaf is then broken. A ritual to express their response to having received the sacrament of the body and blood of Jesus on the Thursday, this bread represents the life lived by Community members during the week. As Augustine of Hippo of the fourth- and fifth-century says, "Be what you can see and receive what you are."[13]

Towards the end of the liturgy, the congregation receives an absolution in words that allow them to enter the Sabbath freed from the burden of guilt or the pressure to produce results in order to be validated by church and wider society. Departing, the gathered are commissioned,

> Today you are absolved from any necessity to provide. No pressure to produce results is to torment you. Today the noise of machinery and the blur of endless words will not trouble you. Not even the power of death. Let no transgression rise up to accuse you. Let go of all that is left undone in the past week. For Christ is risen from the dead, and death cannot trouble us any more.

13. Augustine *Works* 301 (Sermon 272).

Also present in the Sabbath liturgy is a chalice of milk and honey as an icon of the Promised Land. For the Community, these are the joys and promises of the age to come. The service concludes with all greeting each other with words, "Good Sabbath to you," drinking from the chalice filled with milk and honey, and wrapping large portions of the Sabbath bread in a special embroidered cloth, which participants then take to their homes and place on the table where the Sabbath meal will be celebrated. Congregants depart in silence.

In their respective homes, participants uncover the Sabbath bread. The youngest person begins the table service by lighting candles and by saying, "Peace to this house, and all who gather at this table." After a prayer, members pass the bread from one to another. A second prayer follows.

> Your peace, O God, upon this home, and Christ in our midst: in sister and brother, in stranger and friend. Our thanks for each other in Your household. Your grace in our speaking. Your love in our listening. Your joy in our tasting, and all our senses attuned to Your Presence. Amen.

After the meal, participants offer a prayer and close, saying, "For this Sabbath and Your peace, we thank you. Tomorrow [Sunday] we live in the world as Your New Creation. Keep us conscious, honest, simple, and merciful." The people gathered at the table say, "Amen."

On Sundays, during the day, the brothers and sisters come and go for recreation, family outings, or visits. They may simply do nothing! Those whose employment requires working on Sunday try to observe Mondays as a Sabbath day and a Sunday each month with Community members. For example, Brother Andrew serves as pastor of Aberdeen Street Baptist Church, the founding congregation for the original Breakwater Baptist Church. Sister Miriam is pastor at Belmont Uniting Church. As registered nurses, Sister Naomi and Sister Jennie are also on call some Sundays.

Sunday evening is a time of study of scripture and, often, a book that shapes Community reflection and discussion. At the end of the Sabbath, members offer a prayer and close by saying, "For this Sabbath and Your peace, we thank you. Tomorrow [Monday] we live in the world as Your New Creation. Keep us conscious, honest, simple, and merciful."

For years, Breakwater Baptist Church and the Community followed the practice of most Australian Baptists in relation to Sunday morning worship. Decisions to reclaim the Sabbath as an actual day of rest, not just another day to work in a religious way and to cancel formal church activity on Sunday mornings have been important in the life of the Community. HTM has renewed its commitment to the rhythm of Jesus' life, resisted the cultural norm of living faster, no matter what the cost, and drawn closer to Muslim and Jewish friends in the wider community.

Reading scripture during Sabbath service or baptism

At Morning Prayer, members wear a black woolen clerical cloak. Novices and visitors wear a brown one. At the celebration of the Eucharist, members wear their white baptismal albs, received at the time of their baptism with this prayer: "Christ bestow upon this tunic the blessing of Light and upon you may He throw the garment of everlasting salvation and peace." In the Community's hospitality, not just the monastics, but all baptized Christians are invited at the Eucharist to wear the white baptismal alb. Many do.

Aidan Kavanagh's words on the dignity of Baptism have shaped HTM practice:

> Baptism needs more than drops of water, dabs of oil, taps on the cheek, and plasticized bread dipped in a modicum of wine. Baptism into Christ demands enough water to die in, oil so fragrant and in such quantity that it becomes the Easter aroma, kiss-

es and *abrazos* [hugs], bread and wine enough to feed and rejoice hearts. And rooms of glory filled with life rather than crumpled vestments and stacks of folding chairs.[14]

The Community observes what some Baptist circles call *open membership*. This means that participation in the Eucharist is open to everybody; and that someone presenting himself or herself for membership in the Community of the Transfiguration who was baptized as an infant need not go through "re-baptism."

When candidates offer themselves for baptism, they participate in a formal time of preparation known as the Catechumenate. Baptism takes place in Bright Week, the eight days following the Resurrection. The catechumen is immersed three times in water, after which she or he receives the Lord's Prayer, and, after ascending to the top of the steps of the baptistery, is chrismated, or anointed with copious amounts of scented oil. A prayer that "the Spirit will strengthen, guide, empower, and mother all who are baptized in Jesus Christ" accompanies the laying on of hands. Whatever the communion of the candidate may be, the Community invites someone from that denomination—a bishop, superintendent, moderator, senior pastor, or a designated representative—to be present and to officiate at the chrismation with the laying on of hands.

Every year during Holy Week, the entire community participates in a pre-Easter liturgy on Saturday evening by which they renew their baptismal life. By so doing, members acknowledge that baptism is not simply a one-time event, but a model for the Christian life in which we are constantly dying and rising, always being purified and transformed through a process of death, burial, and resurrection, or, in the words of their psycho-spiritual understanding, disintegration, liminality, and integration. Whether baptized in infancy or in adulthood, each member also takes time privately at the baptistery to meditate on the integrity of their baptism and to renew it in the light of their expanding knowledge and experience of God.

The passages that have been quoted from the liturgies enrich understanding of the "prayer of the heart" as experienced by HTM members. At HTM, the life of prayer offers an antidote to an individualized, otherworldly spirituality. Prayer is corporate as well as personal, contemplative

14. Kavanagh, *Shape of Baptism*, 179–80, cited in HTM, "Liturgy for the Renewal of Baptismal Life."

and grounded in ancient tradition, as well as contemporary in its expression. Prayer sustains a journey of ongoing conversion and obedience to God.

Practices for the Common Good

A community of men and women, celibate and married couples, adults and children, HTM has cultivated stable personhood. Of the eighteen professed members living in the Cloister, eleven are celibates and seven are married. Three of the celibates came as divorcees. One brother who lives now as a celibate originally came with his wife and three children. He and his wife lived with the Community, supporting their already failing marriage, while they raised their children together. At a certain point, his wife and he chose to divorce. The wife left the Community while he and the children remained in the Community. The children, the Community, and the mother and father have built new ways of relating well.

The Community has been able to embrace and absorb the unresolved conflict and grief in another long, difficult marriage. With obvious vocations to the contemplative life, the husband and wife, choosing not to divorce, now live out a growing friendship with one another as celibates, while engaging in a healing journey towards self-realization and the hope of ultimate reconciliation.

Betty Drew, a celibate sister, died in the 1980s. Her remains await final committal as the Community has not received permission from the city to create a cemetery or crematorium.

Over the years, people have criticized HTM for a variety of reasons. One source of condemnation has been the matter of divorce. Questions have been raised as to whether the community has been the cause for the breakup when marriages have broken down. In fact, and in contrast with the high rate of divorce in wider Australian society, HTM has nurtured stable marriages. With the two exceptions already mentioned, over twelve couples within the Community of the Transfiguration are in stable, life-long relationships.

HTM has helped raise fourteen children and youth at the Cloister. They are not second-class citizens. They have a charter protecting their rights. They elect a celibate who acts as guardian and advisor. They participate in the life of the Community and are taught many basic life skills that others who grow up outside of a Community often lack.

In personal and group interviews with young people that were raised at the Cloister, I asked what it was like to grow up in the Community. One summarized, "It was great. There was a huge benefit. I learned skills I have applied in my life, in my work, in my marriage: accountability, how to budget and take responsibility for my life, to communicate, to listen. We were respected, our voice counted. I felt I could trust them in all areas to which I was struggling to adjust: spiritual, emotional, and financial."[15]

I asked about restrictions. Of one voice, the young people acknowledged that there were some rules. Those interviewed did not consider the rules to be excessive. For example, they had to observe the rhythm of life in the Cloister and to honor times of silence. They had to respect the right of others to speak. Indeed, the Community requires that only one person speaks at a time. They had to share chores and participate in a liturgy of the Community at least once a week. When they are of high school age, they are limited to a half-hour of television a day or, sometimes, a one-hour program. As a Baptist congregation, HTM does not require baptism, but all the youth have been baptized.

While the monastery has very clearly defined ethics in relation to sex, and specifically to premarital sex, it never imposes its stance on the young people, in this way making them accountable and responsible for their own decisions before God. The young people have very much appreciated and respected this approach. It has also made the crisis between spirituality and sexuality less dangerous for them.

When one of the teenagers living at the Cloister became pregnant to a young man associated with the monastery, the Community explored with both of them and their families a number of options: abortion, adoption, marriage, or living in relationship with one another and raising the child until they reached an age of maturity when they would decide for themselves to marry or not. They chose to live together and raise their child. They received non-judgmental, compassionate, and inclusive assistance, the Community providing a home for them while they completed their schooling. In the end, they did not marry. Going their separate ways, the young man remained single. The young woman married a very remarkable man. The daughter, then fourteen, was in the wedding party.

In terms of finances, the Community looks after all the basic needs of children and youth through their secondary education. Everyone receives pocket money regularly. If a young person continues in post-

15. Interviews with youth: July 10, 2004 and July 24, 2004.

secondary education, the Government of Victoria provides stipends, but the Community continues to offer counsel and material assistance as is needed.

There is no fixed time at which a young person must leave the Cloister. Every member of the Community has a spiritual director. Every young person in the Community has a mentor. The mentor continues to offer guidance as the young person prepares to live outside the Cloister.

One young person, son of members of the Greater Community, has explored making a profession. While supportive, the Community has discouraged the individual from doing so until he has completed his education, established himself in the world, and developed such maturity as would help in making such a decision. The Community has provided him resources such as counseling and employment opportunities.

At times, when indecisiveness has prevented the Community from finding consensus and moving forward together, the Community has consulted the children and youth. On one such occasion, the Community wrestled with the possibility that it would receive into its care people dying of HIV/AIDS. The children broke the deadlock by informing the Community that, regardless of right and wrong, the important thing was "to love them as Jesus does" and to care for them at the Cloister while they died.

Community members generally make decisions by consensus. Typically, members meet briefly each day after Morning Prayer to consider the work for the day, which is set by the Prior, including the care of the sick and those who are to be visited, preparations needed for a happy and peaceful return for those off the grounds, and any other issue. If a minor matter arises during the day, those available meet and settle on what is needed. On less routine issues, every effort is made to involve Skete and Greater Community members living in close proximity to the Cloister.

The Prior may call extraordinary chapter meetings to address an issue, whether minor or major. If the matter is an emergency, the Visitor and Chaplain are informed and invited to be present if they feel it necessary or if they are able. As well, the constitution provides for an annual chapter meeting the Saturday before the Feast of Holy Cross, on September 14. Apart from those living out of Victoria, the whole Community is expected to be present, including the Visitor and Chaplain. The Treasurer provides financial statements and has the monastery books audited for the meeting.

Members living at the Cloister contribute to a common purse in accord with Acts 2:45 and Acts 4:34. All work and give their income to the Treasurers. Members of the Greater Community tithe. Money matters have never become an arena for dispute. At the annual meeting, the Community agrees to a budget which everyone in the Community reviews regularly.

On a daily basis, the Prior and the Treasurer have the major responsibility for money matters. The Prior is an office made functional by two people, and the Treasurer by three people. Members of the "common purse" receive a small amount of personal money every week.

All the members of the Cloister earn some income. Some work in the poorest of circumstances in industry near the Cloister, regardless of academic achievement or prior career choices. This enables them and others to return for the Midday Office and the midday meal at the Cloister. Others work in factories, chaplaincies, education, or health and aged care. In addition to the two clergypersons responsible for congregations, Brothers Stephen and Graeme and Sister Anna all received theological training. One of the founders, Brother Graeme, has pastoral oversight of the community. Brother Steve is co-prior with Brother Stephen who works in the heritage building industry. Sister Anna serves as part-time chaplain at a local school and part-time chaplain at the Geelong Hospital.

Flexibility is a mark of Community life. When there are an unusually high number of visitors, or a number of Community members are away for the day or week, or unanticipated events take place, the Community gives itself permission to sleep in, cancel one of the Offices, or enjoy a day of rest.

Members of the Cloister generally take a month's vacation annually. Those with family abroad are able to travel abroad every four years. On holidays, such as Australia Day, Community members may take an outing together. Or, they may do nothing! Depending on the season, the Community may process tomatoes, apricots, pears, and peaches. While not able to grow all its food, the Community does provide for a significant part of its food supply.

Members respect the beauty of creation. With three buildings set aside for worship specifically, nearly a dozen houses, gardens, and a guest house, the property encompasses almost four acres. The Cloister grounds were once a suburban garbage dump. Now, the Cloister is a protected bird sanctuary.

Summer produce

Out of their contemplative lifestyle, HTM members have under-taken every effort to address the needs of the immediate neighborhood in which they live, as well as wider social issues. In one instance, HTM members helped organize successful resistance to efforts to divert the Barwon River, now a protected reserve. Another successful engagement led to the removal of a nearby motorbike track that was a source of noise pollution. On both occasions, members provided space at the Cloister for meetings. Members participated and joined in delegations to meet with city officials. Both campaigns were win-win situations, and both succeeded. However, HTM and their immediate neighbors have failed to persuade the State of Victoria not to construct a new main road through the middle of the Breakwater suburb.

In the sense that HTM members generally do not join movements, they are not social activists. However, they are certainly socially active and give a place in their lives to participate in movements for peace and justice. Wearing their habits, they have sometimes taken to the streets to protest current federal policies relating to war, refugees, the rights of laborers, and the survival of the environment.

As well, HTM has stood in solidarity with those who are more actively engaged. For example, gracing the Gatehouse in early 2007, a large poster read, "Justice for David Hicks." The United States had detained Hicks, an Australian, at Guantánamo Bay, Cuba, for over five years without trial. In May 2007, Hicks was returned to Australia to complete his sentence.[16]

These examples of seeking to advocate the common good of all who live in the neighborhood, and of protest, point to the approach of HTM members to social issues. Avoiding activism for its own sake, HTM members seek to be conformed to God's image in prayer. Everything is rooted in prayer: work, play, all relationships, and social concerns, everything. The life of prayer of every HTM member relates to every personal, local, and global matter.

Community members begin and end each day together in the Oratory, in silence and stillness. At other times, they dwell with God alone. By prayer and contemplation, they experience intimacy with God. Over time, this has life-changing effects, which dictate the way they are present in a changing society. From a life of prayer to ordinary living, members offer Christian love by their care of those in need in society.

By their lives, HTM brothers and sisters seek to give an example of nonviolent resistance, sanity, integrity, good common sense, and Christian love. Within the Community, members seek to be transparent, to act out of love, and to face difficulties as they arrive. During evening prayer in 2007, they reflect on wisdom gained during a journey of over thirty-five years, as follows:

> We do not turn away from difficulties, distancing ourselves through fear, but we draw near and touch and wrestle with whatever keeps us from loving one another to completion. We are a community that knows deeply that we belong to one another. There is no pace of escape from unlimited evil in a bland suburban heart. We pray

16. Article found on *The Australian's* Web site: http://www.theaustralian.news.com. au/story/0,20867,21690207-2702,00.html.

and work for the well-being of all. We search together for meaning and purpose. We repent of what goes wrong between us. We
act to put things right and make amends. We are alert to signs of
GOD at work in the way we change and the way things are being done, the LORD striving through us to transfigure the realm
of this Community into the realm of Christ. We soberly remember that we are relatively well at other people's expense. We are a
Community where we become more healed by being prepared to
bear more for the sake of those who are less well.

In the early years of the Community of the Transfiguration, people
who had no personal knowledge about the Community, or of monastic
spirituality, generally criticized the brothers and sisters. Many detractors
were decidedly unwilling to visit the Cloister or dialogue with members.

Often, with the help of independent third parties, the Community
has tried to reach out to its critics. In conversation with them, HTM
members have found ways to achieve understanding and reconciliation.
Individuals I have interviewed outside the Community highlight the love
members show for the enemy, critic, or slanderer, those who have offended them, and even those they have offended as a major feature of
HTM's spirituality.

> While monastic life, even in an urban setting, is a counter-cul-
> tural society, it is never a place where people pray *against* or *are
> against* anything or anyone—that is the nature of evil, which must
> never be approached on the basis of its own morality, "Do not
> repay evil with evil." That is why we are called to bless, to pray for,
> and to love the enemy without and within.[17]

Members understand this stance as a practical way to obey Jesus'
teaching about loving the enemy. One consequence has been that, over
time, many of these persons who doubted whether HTM had an authentic place within the Baptist Union of Victoria have now come to support
the Community and to believe that it is of vital importance for the life of
the denomination, both now and in the future.

Community members have not only sought to reach out to critics.
They have also refused to bad-mouth other congregations or to be an un-
intended party to disputes within them. For example, in the mid-1990s,
the Community found itself a source of potential numerical growth and

---

17. *Testament and Pastoral Rule*, 6, emphasis in original.

financial security. More than thirty successful, musically brilliant younger people began to commute each Sunday from Melbourne to Breakwater Baptist Church. Initially, the Community welcomed this sudden influx of visitors. It seemed that God was validating their ministry.

There was a problem. The new attendees represented a faction dissatisfied with their own place of worship. As escapees, they contributed little. They wanted the Community to offer a full Sunday school curriculum, but they were uninterested in rhythm of life of prayer at the Cloister.

Over time, HTM members reflected on two of the temptations of Jesus in the wilderness, those of success as measured by the world, and of financial security (Luke 4:1–13 and parallels). They reflected on the public life of Jesus, often perceived as a failure. His was a path consciously chosen. He emptied himself of all social, religious, and political power. In the desert, he experienced temptation and rejected the offer of success through using power negatively, to manipulate or control others. He chose the right use of power—the power of prayer, of example, and of the one—not the forms of power abused by "powers and principalities" in this world.

Finally, HTM members decided not to be a party to a split within another congregation, but rather to continue to nurture the spiritual and psychological growth of those who had already made Breakwater Baptist Church their spiritual home. As a result, and at the peak of its numerical success, in 2000, the Community cancelled the Sunday morning service of worship and replaced it with the Sabbath service on Saturday evenings.

Transparency and openness in communication are foundational for the life of the Community and are offered as a model and a gift to the church and society at large. HTM members see themselves as an "extreme presence" in the world. Brother Graeme says, "Ours is a spirituality of life that is freely chosen, a path of psychological honesty and transparency."[18]

In practice, this stance of honesty, transparency, and openness enables Community members to be a source of healing and of life for others. In radical witness to the life of God, HTM members share the Gospel not by words as such, but by making Christ present through radical love in the world. Living as monks, HTM members make an impact on many

---

18. Brother Graeme, interview by Paul Dekar, June 26, 2004.

people: critics, seekers, and wounded people who come to them and talk about struggles within their lives. Issues include the breakdown of marriage, sickness, financial problems, problems relating to other workers, and career decisions. It all sounds so commonplace: God is working in extraordinary ways through ordinary people.

Claiming One's Identity as God's Beloved

HTM offers a way of being Christian and a way of being church alternative to the way an overwhelming majority of Christians in Australia and in North America might characterize their experience. HTM sees itself moving towards the renewal of the church and the redemption of the world. However, neither will be accomplished in our lifetime, and so HTM has chosen to remain focused about its vocation, secure in it, and committed to it. At the heart of the life of the Community is the nurture of warm, personal intimacy with the Holy Trinity. This, in turn, enables HTM members to claim their truest identity as God's beloved.

Like the first-century accounts of the life of Jesus, HTM members weave together every key event in Jesus' life: incarnation, baptism, transfiguration, crucifixion, resurrection, and ascension in a rhythm of daily living. By becoming a person, being baptized, living amongst us, and dying, Jesus became one with us in our humanity. By his transfiguration, resurrection, and ascension, Jesus enabled us to share in his divinity, and so to become human beings fully alive as children of God because, "His divine power has given us everything needed for life and godliness, through the knowledge of him who called us by his own glory and goodness. Thus he has given us, through these things, his precious and very great promises . . . and may become participants of the divine nature" (2 Pet 1:4).

HTM members believe in a God who created humanity to be like God. And this reality—"being like God"—always involves us in God's suffering, in the choices that God makes in the presence of evil: choosing to overcome evil with good, never approaching it on the basis of its morality but with the intelligence of the innocent victim. These lessons are learned over a long time. But "being like God" is also sharing in God's light, joy, and peace. One outstanding feature of the monastery's life is its ability to celebrate life with healing extravagance and joy.[19]

19. Alison, *Joy of Being Wrong*, is a major source for these reflections.

A story in Jewish mystical tradition (*kabala*) tells of a dull boy who could not even learn the alphabet. His father did not take him to synagogue, even on the days of awe, for he really was dimwitted. When the boy turned thirteen, of age to receive God's law, the father took him to synagogue on the Day of Atonement that he might not eat something on the day of penance through lack of knowledge or understanding. The boy carried a little whistle that he played whenever he sat in the field and shepherded sheep and cattle. As he sat in the holy place not knowing anything to say when the prayers began, he spoke to his father. "I have my whistle with me. I wish to play on it." The father ordered him not to do so, but the boy persisted. When it was time for the great confession, he could no longer suppress his ecstasy. He tore the whistle from his pocket and let loose. Everyone was bewildered. Slowly, the leader of the community, the great Baal Shem, stood and spoke, "Judgment is suspended, and wrath is dispelled from the face of the earth."[20]

HTM members see everybody as beneficiaries of Jesus' transfiguration. Everybody may hear himself or herself addressed when God said, "This is my Son, the Beloved, listen to him" (Mark 9:7). The glory of the Holy One rests on those who work toward the redemption of the world. With every action, with every service, the *shekina* breaks forth out of its concealment.

HTM members believe that the transfiguration of Jesus is a vision of what happens to humanity when in intimacy it participates in the divine nature. So it is that the glory that emanates from the body of Jesus on the holy mountain and changes his face and clothing reaches out to all creation. It is not so much the revelation of his divinity as a revelation of the glory of a human being fully alive.

Radical love is the heart of HTM spirituality. HTM members love God, self, and others. This has had real significance in their own lives and in the lives of those who come seeking help, God, or something they may not even have been able to name. Making real God's radical love, HTM members nurture in community their own growth, as well as that of friends and visitors who participate in the daily offices or retreats, receive counseling or spiritual direction, or stay as visitors for longer periods of time. One retreatant shared that she lived for a number of weeks at the Cloister during a period of time when she was experiencing a great deal

20. Buber, *Legends of the Baal-Shem*, 30–31.

of difficulty. When asked what she experienced, she replied, "I felt I was cuddled by God."

A number of pastors are among those for whom the Community has provided care. I have interviewed over a dozen pastors who are in professional ministry today and who attribute their longevity in ministry to the Community. Some have come for significant periods of time. Others come regularly simply to spend a quiet day at the monastery.

To offer but one example, a pastor had been dismissed from another denomination because of his expanding theological vision. He was told he would never serve in parish ministry again. In despair, he wandered into the Skete housed at that time at Mt. Waverley, a suburb of Melbourne, where Sister Miriam and Sister Terri, and later the whole community, listened to him and supported him and his family. He was able to change denominations and now serves one of the larger Uniting Church congregations in Australia. In his church building, he has established a space for contemplative prayer modeled on that which provided him sanctuary a decade earlier.

HTM's outstanding quality is the ability of members to create a safe place for healing and journeying to God. In the course of over one hundred interviews with community members, friends, and critics, I have heard amazing stories of the movement from darkness to light, from unhealth to well-being, or from lack of identity to one's True Self. All of this takes place in a social context full of alluring, but ultimately empty, alternatives. From within the daily rhythm of silence, stillness, and prayer, the Holy Spirit touches Community members and visitors, energizing and transfiguring them at every level.

Concluding Reflections

At present, in the North American context, Baptist radicals are much more of a rare breed than were their Baptist forebears. According to historian Martin E. Marty, to imagine Baptists working for peace and justice is something of an oxymoron.[21] Nonetheless, Community of the Transfiguration members are exemplars of a tradition by which many Baptists have offered radical love within church and society. In the name of Jesus, they quite literally feed the hungry, comfort the sorrowful, shel-

---

21. Marty, "Foreword," in Dekar, *For the Healing of the Nations*, xi.

ter the destitute, serve those that mean them harm, and pray for those that persecute them.

Community members consider the monk as "that mysterious archetype—the 'solitary' in every human soul—that like Lazarus is in our baptism made alive and called by the Son of God to 'come forth.'" So, too, do members see themselves today as bound by the grave cloths of the past, yet alive and free. As such, they are a profound sign of life in the midst of a culture of death.[22]

A new way of being Christian is emerging around the world. Members of the Community of the Transfiguration are among those leading the way. Though in my experience members are doctrinally orthodox, their journey has little to do with agreeing to certain doctrines or formulating new ones. Their journey is about heart as well as head. Beloved of God, they respond by loving God and all whom God loves.

In Australia as well as in North America, there is a hunger for a vision of Christianity different from the dominant ways of being Christian so much in the news today. People are far more likely to act their way into right-thinking than to think their way into right-acting. Rather than making categorical or doctrinal statements about Christian faith, members of the Community of the Transfiguration have responded to a call to make manifest the Life of God locally and in the world.[23] An intentional community of people, male and female, married and celibate, members have covenanted to God and to each other to live in such a way that they are transparent with God and with one another. While not professed, birth-children of Community members share in considerable measure in the life of the Community and continue to relate to the Community after they have left from the Cloister to pursue education, career, marriage, or other opportunities.

Words outside the Cloister speak of the community's gratitude, unity, hospitality, and radical love. Through these and other practices, Community members "live their prayers and pray their lives."

---

22. HTM, "Testament and Pastoral Rule," 1–2.

23. HTM, "Baptist Church in Breakwater, 1869–2001," 36.

FOUR

Theology of the Resolve

In this chapter, we explore the commitments members of HTM articulate in their Resolve. Not a rule, not a set of laws, the Resolve is an instrument for following the Gospel and growing in Christ-likeness. The Resolve distills practices by which Community members have come to share life together over the past thirty-five years. To give the text as a whole again, in 2007 the Resolve reads as follows:

> Being perfectly assured of your salvation, with your whole life proclaim your gratitude.
>
> Reject nothing, consecrate everything.
>
> Be the good of love, for God, for neighbour, for all creation.
>
> Judge no one, not even yourself.
>
> Love beauty.
>
> Maintain inner-silence in all things.
>
> Show hospitality; err only on the side of generosity.
>
> Speak truth to power, especially power without love.
>
> Let your only experience of evil be in suffering, not its creation.
>
> For us there is only the trying, the rest is none of our business.

No single sentence of the Resolve has priority for the Community. As Community members have reflected on their understandings of the Resolve, they have emphasized that everything flows from a sense that God infuses everything with a gracious presence. Renewing all things,

God is a constant source of strength and joy. Community members respond with gratitude that is deeply rooted and fruitful.

THE PRACTICE OF GRATITUDE

"Being perfectly assured of your salvation,
with your whole life proclaim your gratitude."

This opening line of the Resolve integrates a major tenet of the sixteenth-century Protestant reformers that salvation is by God's grace alone, *sola gratia,* and the Orthodox Christian emphasis on synergy or deification. Orthodox teaching is consistent with texts such as Phil 2:12–13, 2 Cor 3:17–18, and 2 Pet 1:4, as well as with classic Protestant teaching summarized in an article that explores the thought of John Calvin.

> The task of the image is to deify (*deificare*) the children of God and to transform the world. Christ is the prototype. He "rose for the purpose of making us . . . partakers of the same glory with Himself." The chief instrument of transfiguration is the Gospel, the end of which is "to render us eventually conformable to God, and, if we may so speak, to deify us." The change refers not to "essence but quality" in order to preserve the distinction between creator and creature. We are made to "conform to God, not by an inflowing of substance, but by the grace and power of the Spirit . . . who surely works in us without rendering us consubstantial with God." Although we have "participation in God," it is "Christ alone" who "has an *imago* relation in substance to God, [people] only by irradiation." . . . Not only humanity is to be transfigured. "The elements of the world . . . are to be consumed, only that they may be renovated, their substance still remaining the same."[1]

Gratefulness is the energizing source of Benedictine spirituality, an approach to life in fullness. The starting point is listening, or, in other words, being awake and mindful. The *Rule of Benedict (RB,* Prologue) opens with these words,

> Listen carefully, my child, to the master's instructions, and attend to them with the ear of your heart. This is advice from a parent who loves you; welcome it, and faithfully put it into practice. . . . Let us open our eyes to the light that comes from God, and our

---

1. Copper, "Theology of Image in Eastern Orthodoxy and John Calvin," 233–34. Citations from Calvin's writings in the original text.

ears to the voice from heaven that every day calls out. . . . "Run while you have the light of life, that the darkness of death may not overtake you." (John 12:35)

Commenting on these lines, Benedictine sister Joan Chittister writes,

> Our entire generation has gone deaf. Scripture and wisdom and relationship and personal experience are all being ignored. We are, consequently, a generation of four wars and of the most massive arms buildup in the history of the world—in a period called peacetime. We are a generation of great poverty in the midst of great wealth, of great loneliness in the center of great communities; of serious personal breakdowns and community deterioration in the face of unparalleled social growth; of great spiritual ennui in the middle of our great claims of being a God-fearing country.

In our spiritual wasteland, she observes, we need to recover a spirituality of the open heart, a willingness to be touched, and a sense of gratefulness.[2]

According to Cistercian Brother David Steindl-Rast, gratitude is not simply an emotion, but one way of experiencing the life of the Triune God within us. This life springs from the Creator, fountain and wellspring of divinity, the ultimate Giver. And this is how God prays, "by dancing. It is one great celebration of belonging by giving and thanksgiving. We can begin to join that dance in our heart right now through gratefulness. What else could be called life in fullness?"[3]

During the 1930s, Grandchamp in French-speaking Switzerland became the meeting place of the *Dames de Morges*, a group of women in the Reformed tradition who sought to deepen their experience and understanding of the Christian faith through occasional spiritual retreats. In response to a renewed liturgical life in the Protestant churches, the community developed a form of daily office that became the basis of the *Office of Taizé*, the prayer book used today for common prayer at Grandchamp. Mère Geneviève Micheli, leader of the community from 1944 up until her death in 1961, affirmed that prayer is a grateful response to God's grace. In a message on "The Witness of a Community of Prayer," she chose the transfiguration of Christ as the paradigm of a contemplative community.

2. Chittister, *Wisdom Distilled from the Daily*, ch. 2.
3. Steindl-Rast, *Gratefulness, the Heart of Prayer*, 189.

> Today, Christians need to trust in the salvation of humanity, the pledge of the Spirit, and the coming of the Kingdom. They are called to glorify God. This is the witness of the community that prays. For those who pray are called by Christ to go up the Mountain of the Transfiguration.[4]

In the experience of grace, a Christian undergoes a kind of transfiguration in her or his daily life. Enzo Bianchi of the Bose Community in Italy describes this as the world giving itself to us. In response, we enter into life in joyful gratitude.[5] By contrast with this emphasis in monastic spirituality, many Christians' experiences in the church's life consist in working hard for God but not having time to be with God, speaking for God but not listening to God, and pushing agenda on God's behalf while there is little interest in being in communion with the God in whose name Christians evangelize. The culture of church life as many have known it fosters knowledge about God but does not satisfy the deepest longing in the heart to know God in intimacy, as the Hebrew word *yada* connotes.

Many HTM members came to the Community of the Transfiguration with such an unfulfilled background in the church. Most of them were active within their original denominations and congregations. It was not easy for them to move to a new place of residence where they could pray, read scripture, and share their experience of the grace of God as the primary source of assurance of salvation and as the foundation of a new spiritual home.

At HTM, nothing members do is about earning salvation. They do not work for God. Rather, they respond to God with gratitude. The following words guide Community members: "Turn and train yourself to live in a constant state of gratitude for all things. For from gratitude is born respect, and from respect—reverence, and by reverence you will protect and preserve all the Creator's work."[6]

Members experience the grace of the triune God as the primary source of energy for daily living. By the life, death, and resurrection of Jesus, members are being conformed to Christ's likeness from one degree of glory to another (2 Cor 3:18). In response, members share Good News

---

4. Clifford, "Protestant Monastic Community of Grandchamp," 234.
5. Bianchi, *Worlds of Spirituality*, 114.
6. *Testament and Pastoral Rule*, 54.

that God has become one with humankind in our humanity, including our suffering.

A secondary source of gratitude is the experience of being part of a community characterized by contemporary spiritual writer and educator Parker Palmer as a circle of trust, a communal place of safety that welcomes the soul, helps members to hear its voice, and reclaims what Thomas Merton called "a hidden wholeness." Integrity comes from knowing one's truest self.[7]

HTM offers assurance of salvation in part by the way community members respond to each other and to every person. This reinforces the saving influence on them of changes in their lives, their relationships with one another, and their growth in transparency. By their responses to every person, HTM members witness that salvation is indeed happening. They see and experience it in each person. Members challenge any negative self-doubt or self-destructiveness and reflect the mind of Christ to each other.

Life in community nurtures members in a lifelong process of transfiguration into the life of Christ (Rom 12:1–2). God is manifest in the lives of members who seek to live holy lives by following the self-emptying pattern of Jesus (Phil 2:6–11), that is the fact that Jesus relinquished all divine attributes to experience human suffering. Community members see this as a way to live out their baptism. Salvation is not an ethereal concept focused on the hereafter. Rather, Community members experience new birth in events or processes such as joy and human fulfillment by liberation from events of the past and their imprisoning or paralyzing impact, the stabilizing of emotions, the healing of broken human sexuality, the opening up of human life for relationship and intimacy with God and others, and freedom from a sacrificial theology that breeds self-destruction or scapegoating.

Community members experience salvation in the here and now. "Whoever has the Son has life" (1 John 5:12). "And this is eternal life, that they may know you, the only true God, and Jesus Christ whom you have sent" (John 17:3). HTM members let their whole lives speak. Who they are and what they do in every aspect of their lives, not just what they say,

---

7. Palmer, *Hidden Wholeness*, 22. Palmer quotes Merton's poem *Hagia Sophia*, in McDonnell, *Thomas Merton Reader*, 506.

attest that they are disciples of Jesus. Proclaiming the Gospel in all of life, members use words only when necessary.

All phrases of the Resolve yield to the priority of gratitude: the way Community members make moral decisions; how they deal with despair, pathology, betrayal, disputes, and suffering; how they share possessions; how they nurture loving relationships; how they create and maintain beautiful grounds out of what was a local rubbish dump; how they show themselves to be serious about unity, truth, and goodness; and how they offer hospitality. Everything is a response of gratitude to God. Union with God radiates into all of life. Doing comes out of being a new creation in Christ.

Often the outer environment is a parable of what has taken place on the inside. This is evident at HTM. Members are grateful not only for what God did two thousand years ago, but also for their experience of God today. They express this in worship. During their Saturday liturgy, members, Companions, and friends freely express gratitude for the ways God has been present to them in daily life during the week past.

> *All:* Like Jesus, Let us be fools in this world.
>
> *Cantor:* In facing the future
>
> *A:* let us never abandon Him [Jesus Christ] or others.
>
> *C:* In facing the truth
>
> *A:* may we find freedom from illusion.
>
> *C:* In accepting wounds
>
> *A:* may we know the way to healing and wholeness.
>
> *C:* In embracing the scapegoated
>
> *A:* may we know our own redemption.
>
> *C:* In discovering our true selves
>
> *A:* may we abandon self-destruction.
>
> *A:* In seeking adult innocence
>
> *C:* may we no longer harm.
>
> *A:* In yielding to dying
>
> *C:* may we know love's pain and joy.
>
> *A:* In the folly of Jesus' life
>
> *C:* May we find our own.
>
> *C:* Fools to our society

Diognetus 5

A: we know the Wisdom of God.

C: Unknown

A: we cannot be ignored.

C: Dying

A: we still live on.

C: Disciplined by suffering

A: we are not beaten down.

C: Knowing sorrow

A: we always have cause for joy.

C: Emptying ourselves

A: we make others rich.

C: Owning nothing

A: we are given the world.

C: Grateful for every breath

A: life becomes a precious gift.

THE PRACTICE OF CONSECRATING ALL OF LIFE

"Reject nothing, consecrate everything."

By the second phrase of the Resolve, the sisters and brothers express their determination to become "inviolably vulnerable," a concept from the ancient Syrian church.[8] Without vulnerability, the experience of God, life, and others will be very limited. Honoring the need for some measure of privacy in some areas, HTM members attempt to practice discernment with a basic attitude of openness and acceptance and to preserve inner peace and stability when the unexpected, the undeserved, or the unwanted threatens the individual or Community by its sudden appearance.

To reject nothing demands a considerable degree of psychological and spiritual maturity, a willingness to suffer the stress of holding opposites together without resolving the tension by getting rid of or rejecting either the one or the other, or mixing them together. Above all, it means coming to terms with the personal shadow of the individual and collective lives of members, and of the life of the world.

By personal shadow, members understand that aspect of life that is unexpressed, unseen, hidden, unacceptable, and usually unconscious.

8. Ross, *Fountain and Furnace*, 15.

The shadow can, and indeed must, be brought into consciousness. It is not evil. Psychologist Carl Jung (1875–1961) taught that perhaps only 10 percent of the shadow is evil. The rest contains many treasures needed to balance the personality and that are essential for integration into wholeness.[9]

For Community members, the integration and consecration of the shadow is a moral concern. The shadow longs for incarnation. Members seek to recognize both the glory and the demonic darkness of it, and to bring it to the light of God. They seek to understand what is repressed, feared, rejected, hated, and despised, and how they project what is repressed onto others and the creation around them. Community members keep a watchful eye for such negative behavior. Committed to transparency, they seek to avoid rationalizing away any form of self-deception or to project their shadow, or false self by lying, hurting, maiming, manipulating, scapegoating or otherwise abusing others.

The healing of the shadow is an issue of love. Loving self is not easy. For HTM members, Jesus taught loving all of oneself, even negative feelings towards the enemy, the inferior, the socially unacceptable. Any evidence of intractable weakness, stubbornness, willful blindness, cruelty, meanness, sham, pride, or readiness to sacrifice another's life and welfare to secure one's own comfort is confessed, amended, and forgiven.

To love one's self is not to be permissive or to condone dark, destructive energies within. To love self begins by carrying all this consciously and by accepting the discomforting pain of humiliation. As members come to accept or contain the negative or rejected parts of their shadow, such as ego-obsession, they experience self-knowledge and humility in the presence of God, who helps them become strong in love. Learning to love and help themselves, the positive aspects of the shadow help in immediate living, bearing fruit that lasts, and salvation. HTM members love God and others more. During the season of Pentecost in 2007, words of the Evening Prayer address what kind of love Community members seek to exemplify as follows:

> To act out of love and be willing to carry the suffering which the good and true must inevitably bear in a world like ours—in a world which is only partly divine and which must be won for God through grace and human effort—that is the deepest utterance of

9. Hillman, "The Inner Darkness: The Unconscious as a Moral Problem."

all the Prophets and the Law, and the culminating ideal of Jesus'
life and true prayer.

To own one's shadow allows members no comfortable hiding place
in either their inner world or their life in community. Members cannot be
with the poor from an insulated high-rise building in a city. To be a healing presence with a pure heart in wider society, they suffer the tension
and contradictions of living with the rejected, violent, unredeemed parts
of their lives in community. Before undertaking social action, members
seek first to disarm the human heart, essential for personal transformation and nonviolent living.[10]

To consecrate is to set apart for a holy use. For example, one makes
a conscious, intelligent, and educated choice to use the energy of anger
not in the service of evil but of compassion. To consecrate such a source
of energy or capacity is to re-direct it in the service of God and of others. Stubbornness becomes persistence, and perfectionism becomes the
careful creation of beauty. In these and other ways, members re-channel
energy that can otherwise manifest itself in evil back to God, who works
all things for good.

THE PRACTICE OF LOVE

"Be the good of love, for God, for neighbour, for all creation."

The Biblical emphasis on love is crucial to the monastic spirituality of
the Community. We are first of all to love the Lord our God with all our
hearts, souls, and minds; and to love our neighbors as ourselves (Matt
22:37–39 and parallels; *RB* 4.1). Loving begins with God. "In this is love,
not that we loved God but that He loved us" (1 John 4:10). To be the good
of love for God is to respond spontaneously, immediately, passionately,
and vulnerably to God's love.

Love can be harmful, manipulative, smothering, deceiving, self-
serving, or violent. Self-knowledge allows one to face manipulative,
smothering, deceived, and self-serving aspects of love. These are among
the many ways by which people abuse others in the name of love to gain
something for themselves. This is why Community members are alert to
signs of God at work in the ways they change, the ways the Lord is striv-

---

10. Brother Graeme, "Festival Letter—Epiphany 2005," 6.

ing through them to transfigure the realm of the Community and of the world into the realm of Christ.

Jesus asked a man who had been ill for thirty-eight years, "Do you want to be made well?" (John 5:6). In some sense as a response to this question, Christians have often characterized church and monastery as places of convalescence and healing. For example, Thomas Merton described monasticism as a way to overcome self-absorption and ill-health. The day he died in Bangkok, he said to Buddhist and Christian monks,

> Both Christianity and Buddhism agree that the root of man's problems is that his consciousness is all fouled up and he does not apprehend reality as it fully and really is; that the moment he looks at something, he begins to interpret it in ways that are prejudiced and pre-determined to fit a certain wrong picture of the world, in which he exists as an individual ego in the center of things. . . . [S]cholars like Jung, and people of the Jungian school, and those psychologists and patristic scholars who meet, for example, at the Eranos meeting annually in Switzerland . . . understand the vital importance and dynamism of myth as a psychological factor in man's adaptation to reality. . . . So our myth of original sin, as explained for example by St. Bernard, comes very close indeed to the Buddhist concept of avidya, of this fundamental ignorance. Consequently, Christianity and Buddhism look primarily to a transformation of man's consciousness—a transformation, and a liberation of the truth imprisoned in man by ignorance and error. . . . You find, for example, the Cistercians of the 12th century speaking of a kind of monastic therapy. . . . The period of monastic formation is a period of cure, of convalescence. When one makes one's profession, one has passed through convalescence and is ready to begin to be educated in a new way . . . the whole purpose of the monastic life is to teach men to live by love.[11]

HTM members intentionally seek to choose the good of love rooted in the self-emptying love of Jesus. Jungian Sibylle Birkhauser-Oeri writes, "One must not forget that it is impossible to love others so long as one does not know oneself. Sentimentality is not love; it is a state of ignorance of one's shadow. Only conscious eros has healing power."[12]

Community members seek to be the good of love for neighbour in joy and hurt, success and struggle, good times and those of special

11. Merton, *Asian Journal*, 332–33.
12. Birkhauser-Oeri, *The Mother*, 94.

need, as when conflict, ill-health, unemployment, surgery or death intrudes, and also in the ordinary flow of life. Returning one night from the funeral of a relative of a Community member, Brother Neil thought he noticed a woman whose car had a flat tire. As driver, Brother Neil turned around, and the party offered to help. When the spare proved as flat as the tire to be replaced, the Community members offered to take the tire several miles to be repaired. "You would do this for a stranger?" asked the woman. "Why not?" replied Brother Neil.

Sometimes, Community members express love of neighbor in social and justice engagement locally and in the wider world. Community members seek to be an extreme presence not by violence that separates and isolates but by compassionate, inclusive love, especially for the personal and collective enemy. To be the good of love for creation leads members to seek to care for the environment, to create and protect beauty, and to reverence all life.

To be the good of love is to know we are not alone in life. God is present not only in silence, stillness, and solitude, but also in the way God is present through one another. The moment we cease to hold each other, the moment we break faith with one another, the sea engulfs us and the light goes out.

THE PRACTICE OF NOT JUDGING

"Judge no-one, not even yourself."

Community members understand judging as condemnation or being pharisaic by separating oneself from others as a result of thinking oneself better than others. To be non-judgmental is not an attempt to escape self-knowledge or self-confrontation, neither does it condone nor cooperate with unethical behavior in ourselves or others. Rather, it means compassionate understanding of others and of the unredeemed, lawless parts of life. Jesus calls us not to reject and consign to Hell, but to love and transfigure. We can be genuinely non-judgmental only if we personally own, name, and embrace the edges of our own destructive affectivity. We discern the same destructive elements in ourselves that we see in others out there. As we own these elements, we cease to project them onto others.

In order not to judge, the human heart must first be disarmed. The acceptance of personal evil and darker self-knowledge can only take place in a safe environment that does not limit anyone's capacity to own, name, and embrace needed work for change and inner peace. This is why members make ample room for contemplative prayer. A rhythm of life rooted in silence, stillness, and solitude allows members to contemplate the attitude that God has towards us in the incarnation. God so identified with humanity that the Divine Self became one with humankind in order that we might share in the God-self.

Jesus wants us to live what he taught and modeled. We are to embrace the enemy within and without. Accepting all that is within us, we allow Christ to convert and transfigure our inner violence and rage. In grateful response, we in turn love God, self, and the other, even our enemy.

Not to judge means the acceptance of suffering, not the avoidance of it. Benedict included bearing injuries patiently among the "tools for good works" (RB 4:29–33).[13] For Benedictine Sister Joan Chittister, this "peacemaker's paragraph" is the centerpiece of the monastic life. Self-acceptance releases energy and a loving quality in everything members do and it gives life, hope, and a sense of endless new beginning. The self-knowledge gained in contemplation allows members to get in touch with one of the most powerful inner entities: the power to destroy ourselves and others. Members accept the legitimate suffering and pain of this knowledge, and the stress of the ensuing inner battle against acceptance where the struggle to love as Christ loved is waged.

Putting these ideas into practice cannot be done in isolation. Evil is that strong. Disarming the heart is that challenging. Community members rely on two things principally: an experience of a Spirit that is greater than the spirit of evil; and a warm human community, "C. G. Jung once aptly commented that only two things could keep a person's soul from falling under the power of evil: if a person's soul is filled with a power greater than the power of evil; or if a person is contained in a warm, related human community."[14] Monica Furlong makes a related point when she writes, "Wholeness demands relationship with man [sic] or with God, and often with both together."[15]

One knows God through others. To judge another is to do violence to that person, and to the Christ in the other. To judge oneself does violence not only to oneself, but also to others because we are all intercon-

---

13. Chittister, *Rule of Benedict*, 51.

14. Sanford, *Evil*, 109.

15. Furlong, *Travelling In*, 64.

nected. Jesus has compassion for people. Learning compassion for self, members learn compassion for others. As members have dealt with their own shadow-self, they have claimed a new freedom to embrace the enemy without in radical love.

While the Community does not judge, it does discriminate. This means feeling the tension of the opposites within us, good and ill, love and hate. Without running away, members seek to discern what is right and what is good. In contemplation members have time for this choice; in community, members experience safety on the journey, even while the enemy continues to disturb and destroy. And so repentance, self-forgiveness, and radical love for God, self, and others flourish in an excess of time and space.

The spirituality of the Community of the Transfiguration is not otherworldly. Members suffer the tension and sorrow of waiting, the struggle of joy-making sorrow that is worth-while now. It is the way of Jesus. Community members have said yes to it, and they extend the practice of not judging themselves to not judging others. Many visitors to the Cloister come bearing not only pain inflicted on them, but also self-inflicted wounds. Community members provide counsel and even advice, but not judgment.

To offer but a single example, a minister, prominent in his denomination, came to the Community in the company of a woman, similarly prominent in her denomination. Both were married and on the cusp of an affair. Community members were assigned to listen and to offer spiritual direction to each of them while they were at the Cloister. After a period of time, the Community offered the couple one hundred dollars. This would cover a room at a local hotel, at which they might consummate their affair; or a meal at a restaurant, at which they might agree not to do so. The couple enjoyed the meal and returned to their families. In an interview with me, the pastor shared the power of the Community's nonjudgmental witness.

THE PRACTICE OF LOVING BEAUTY

"Love Beauty."

This fifth practice of the Resolve draws on the idea that beauty will save the world, and nothing is as beautiful as Christ.[16] Another source of the

---

16. Dostoevsky, "From the life of the Elder Zossima," *Brothers Karamazov*, 340.

phrase is *The Philokalia*, which means love of the beautiful. Love of beauty is a window onto the beauty of Christ, the exalted, the excellent, understood as the transcendent source of life and the revelation of Truth.[17]

Path to courtyard

Cloister walk

17. Palmer, Sherrard, and Ware, "Introduction," *Philokalia*, 1, 13.

Believing that, when the beauty of Christ attracts us, we turn from an unhealthy love of self and towards a healthy love of the life of Christ within ourselves and within others, HTM members express their love of beauty in a comprehensive way. The grounds, the places where Community members gather for worship or arrange flowers, work space, personal rooms, and table settings all speak of God's grace and beauty and means by which God's presence is known. The love of beauty feeds, strengthens, and brings joy to the soul. It reaches deep into human beings. It creates a resonance, a vibration within. It generates energy, unseen yet felt, and calls for response. "Beauty does not linger, it only visits. Yet beauty's visitation affects us and invites us into its rhythm, it calls us to feel, think, and act beautifully in the world: to create and live a life that awakens the Beautiful."[18]

The love of beauty is a strong challenge to a negative self-image and calls those who worship to find the beauty of one's own being, the lost treasure, the Christ-Self. A liturgy puts it this way, "O Christ You came forth to restore our ancient destiny and renew our ancient beauty."[19]

Love of beauty allows for the invisible to be made visible and makes room for the non-utilitarian pursuits of the composer, craftsperson, dancer, poet, performer, and musician to create a quality of life and of the environment that evokes ever-growing gratitude for, and ever-deepening contemplation of the beauty of Christ. All visitors to HTM attest to the beauty they experience there. This contrasts with a culture that does not have a God-centered understanding of beauty. As a result, society creates many new things that are ugly, sterilized, and violent. By contrast, HTM members create beauty rooted in the true beauty of Christ. This attitude generates respect by which HTM members approach every person as beloved of God and the manner by which HTM members think about art, film, literature, music, utilitarian pursuits, and worldview.

THE PRACTICE OF INNER PRAYER

"Maintain inner silence in all things."

According to Benedict, we are all to listen readily to holy reading and devote ourselves often to prayer (*RB* 4:55). The sixth sentence of the Resolve characterizes inner prayer as the practice of the presence of God, title of

18. O'Donohue, *Beauty*, 13.
19. HTM, "Noon Office," Monday through Friday.

a seventeenth-century book by the French Carmelite Nicholas Herman, known largely by his monastic name, Brother Lawrence. The whole point of being mindful of God in prayer and in the regular reading of the Bible is to listen to God. One learns always to be conscious of God in one's soul.

Consciously, members of HTM understand that they are bearers of the divine image. All the acting, speaking, and creativity of members come out of an intuitive awareness of God within. To know that the "deep, abiding, fertile, healing stillness" they experience is actually God present within them,[20] Community members take seriously the quieting of the body and of the mind as a spiritual discipline. To maintain inner stillness and awaken the imagination, some use aids such as listening, rituals, silence, solitude, and a psycho-spiritual approach to understanding dreams.

Maintaining inner silence in all things is an essential element for any pilgrim, a continual learning that increases in intensity through life's journey. Understanding that a Christian will never arrive at that goal in this life, members nonetheless practice mental, emotional, and physical stillness. Though easier to do with others than alone, members do seek out solitude.

Inner silence is a state of active attention, not a blank. It is a listening to the voice of God. Inner silence is being sensitized to a compassionate, inclusive response to injustice. Community members attempt not to repay evil with evil or set themselves against evil as it has set itself against what is good. Above all, members of the Community of the Transfiguration value interior prayer. Its blessings are silence and stillness in all vicissitudes of life. Only love for Christ Jesus can sustain us in this practice to the end of our earthly journey.[21]

THE PRACTICE OF HOSPITALITY

"Show hospitality, err only on the side of generosity."

According to Jim Cotter, an Anglican priest based in the United Kingdom, the word "hospice" originally referred to places of rest, food, and conviviality offered to pilgrims, travelers, strangers, and those in need. In contrast with contemporary North American usage, which associates

20. HTM, "Sabbath Liturgy."

21. HTM, "Testament and Pastoral Rule," 54.

hospice care with dying, the earlier idea of hospice care was rooted in monastic spirituality.[22]

In the sense of hospice care as offering hospitality, HTM rightly characterizes itself as a Baptist hospice. The Community looks not only to traditional monasteries as model, but also to Ephrata, the eighteenth-century non-resistant (or pacifist) community in Lancaster County, Pennsylvania. During the winter of 1777–1778, Ephrata allowed the Cloister to serve as a hospital for soldiers in the revolutionary army. One patient described his experience as follows, "Many a poor fellow, who entered there profane, immoral, and without hope or God in the world, left it rejoicing in the Saviour."[23]

HTM articulates its experience of salvation as the hospitality of God who embraces all humankind within the Life of the Holy Trinity. The Community cites Jesus' words to Zacchaeus, "I must stay in your house today" (Luke 19:5) and George Herbert's poem *Love (III)*, "Love bade me welcome" as expressing the idea of God welcoming us, an experience of salvation on earth in the here-and-now.[24]

The incarnation is for our inclusion. God invites us to share in the fullness of the Divine Life and empowers us to dwell in God, for God is in us. Hospitality offers healing power that builds a bridge between enemies, between abusers and their victims, between different faith traditions, political traditions, and sexual orientations.

HTM's hospitality includes generous use of Community finances, gifts, time, and material possessions. Members have abandoned any temptation to profane these graces by using them for their own ends. By generous hospitality, they manifest the ecstatic love of God to all they can take into their hearts, emotions, and being. HTM has nurtured some persons for years.

In 2006 alone, HTM received forty-five hundred visitors, and over six hundred bed-nights. Visitors included theological students from Baptist and Uniting Church in Australia teaching institutions, ecumenical groups, senior students from Christian secondary schools in Geelong, sociology and psychology students from Deakin University, groups of

22. Cotter, *Love Rekindled, Practicing Hospitality*, 1; Cotter, e-mail to Paul Dekar, July 13, 2004.

23. Ephrata Cloister, broadsheet commemorating the 225th anniversary of the United States War for Independence.

24. George Herbert, *The Country Parson, The Temple*, 316.

clergy, inter-faith groups, and hundreds of other persons. Guests attended the daily offices and liturgies, days of reflection, and varied celebrations. The Community fed visitors, and gave them gifts.

Generally, visitors report having been enriched by the hospitality of the Community and deeply moved by a sense of the presence of God. A recent visitor, Debbie Ryman, described her experience at HTM as "a hundred percent care." The hospitality of our brothers and sisters has, at times, overwhelmed my wife Nancy and me.

 To summarize this practice, members proclaim the Gospel through hospitality and generosity. These are among the most tangible forms of HTM's radical love. By generous hospitality, HTM members witness to the ecstatic love of the Holy Trinity that they have experienced, and extend that love to all whose paths are joined with theirs.

THE PRACTICE OF TRUTH-TELLING

"Speak truth to power, especially power without love."

As disciples of Jesus, HTM members seek to deal with destructive, loveless power, within and without, by humble love. While they empty themselves, even for the enemy, what do they do if enemies do not change, but resist love? Rather than resorting to force or violence, cutting off an offending member or entity to safe-guard the community, or ignoring problems, members speak truth to power.

This is much harder than the alternatives. To speak truth to power preserves integrity and leaves an open door for an offending power to acknowledge truth, repent, and change. A basic HTM commitment is to radical honesty about the self, transparency, revealing thoughts to a trusted person, and bringing into the open anything that troubles or disturbs the peace that Christ imparts to each person and to the community. Speaking the truth in their liturgical life, notably, members break the power of secrecy. Persons in HTM are freed from the paralyzing hold of unconfessed attitudes or behaviors that otherwise infest and secretly poison community life. The Eucharistic Liturgy states, "Lord, You have told us that hidden deceit saps the source of our communion with You."

In the clearest and most compassionate ways possible, members name truth as they see it. This gives them a power not of violence or coercion but of truth, which can set free those who speak it and, ideally, those who hear it. Even if the other does not hear, accept, or receive the truth, members believe they have done their best and are now free to suffer consciously, willingly, and knowingly whatever ill the other is doing. Suffering evil, they believe they are manifesting the love of God. This gives them a sense of dignity and a deep peace even in the midst of the stress caused by living with what is hostile and unredeemed. In their Prayer of Approach they pray,

> In the name of God
> In the name of Jesus
> Come out of darkness into the light
> that we may understand and withstand you,
> that we may know your name and nature
> that you may cease your hold on us and
> wound us no more.
> Striving with you in the love of God,
> may you come to yield your energy in
> the service of healing life and making it whole,
> transfigured by the power of that love that
> is deeper than the deepest pain . . .
> However much you are held at bay,
> your power of destruction lurks.
> I cannot expel you, conquer, defeat or destroy you.
> We belong together,
> we live and die together,
> are bound Hell-ward or heavenward together.
> I may have to say to you, "Hold your distance, Stay in your own
>   place."
> I may have to bind you.
> Perhaps you are open to change,
> to transfiguration.
> Perhaps you could become my ally
> in the purpose of a greater good.
> If you struggle to take over and run riot in my emotions,
> my mind, my body,
> if you resist all love—you cannot destroy me.
> In yourself you are power without love
> and love will triumph over mere power.

> Love alone will take you, calm and soothe you of your violence
> and transfigure you.[25]

Crucial aspects of the Community's commitment to truth-telling are the accountability, transparency, and vulnerability of its members. From one of its earliest liturgies, the Community affirms, "We believe that life can be radically different." Together with gratitude, compassion, love of beauty, and generous hospitality, another aspect of the Community's radical love has been its commitment for over thirty-five years to creating safe space for the work of healing that takes place within a context of truth telling.[26]

THE PRACTICE OF INNOCENT SUFFERING

"Let your only experience of evil be in suffering, not its creation."

The ninth phrase of the Resolve accepts that there is no escape from the knowledge of evil. Recalling Gen 3:22, Community members acknowledge that humans have become "like one of us [God], knowing good and evil." Humans are now responsible for choices made. This is a daily practical reality for anyone living in any community of faith and indeed for any human being. We are called not to reject the dark side of the human soul. We are clearly called to discriminate and to choose what is good, what is right, neither to perpetrate evil, nor to cooperate with it by silence or passivity.

As long as humans make the error of imagining that evil can be done away with by amputation, coercion, or total war, we will inevitably create more evil. It is in the nature of evil to be against something. If we set ourselves against evil, we will become like it by using its methods and terms. We will create more evil in the very attempt to eradicate it. Rather, "suffering and evil must be combated by means of participation."[27] It is the nature of the Word of God to be "for" and not "against," to save and not destroy. "I am God and no mortal, the Holy One in your midst, and I will not come in wrath" (Hos 11:9). To save rather than destroy, God chooses

25. A prayer by the Community in collaboration with Jim Cotter.

26. Michael King, OSB, Abbot of St. Mark's Abbey, Camperdown, interview by Paul Dekar, June 10, 2004; Dr. Tom Patterson, community therapist, Relationship Centre, Melbourne, interview by Paul Dekar, June 29, 2004; Jim Cotter, e-mail to Paul Dekar, July 13, 2004.

27. de Beausobre, *Creative Suffering*, v.

to suffer. God does not perpetrate evil, but experiences evil by suffering, and in this way wrestles with it and overcomes it. The victory of Christ is not that of a warrior with a sword but that of a wrestler who stands her or his ground. The One who harrows Hell is the Crucified One, covered with wounds but undiminished in mercy and compassion.[28]

Living in community is the spiritual discipline in which this choice is practiced and that makes it possible to make this choice. Without a faithful human community, we could be destroyed by the experience of evil. Knowing that we belong to the Body of Christ and are participating in his sufferings as we make the same choices he made, we are sustained. In community and identification with his sufferings, HTM members experience an increased intensity in their awareness of his presence.

To choose to suffer rather than create more evil is neither to glorify suffering for its own sake, nor to make mileage out of being a victim; nor need it imply stoicism or the shutting down of feelings; nor indeed the suppression of manifestations of anger or grief. If nothing is felt, nothing is suffered, then nothing and no one is loved either. Suffering is redemptive only if it is consciously chosen, willingly accepted and felt, for the sake of the good of love. "No one takes [my life] from me, but I lay it down of my own accord" (John 10:18). HTM members display courage and love, recognized in this liturgy:

> Let us not forget our faithfulness and its cost.
> Let us not forget our suffering—for others' benefit, for another's redemption.
> Let us not forget that what is lacking in Christ's sufferings in the church is made up in our pain.
> Do not forget your suffering or dismiss its significance for the transfiguration of the world.
> Let us not forget that some people become voluntary pain-bearers absorbing the anger and hurt of others and giving back acceptance and care.
> Their love creates the environment for healing change.[29]

In choosing this way, members have found a deep peace beyond all anguish, the peace of Jesus who "is as near the tempted mind as He

28. HTM, "Saturday Noon Office."

29. HTM, "Evening Prayer and Testimony for the Season of the Transfiguration of Our Lord."

is to the broken heart."[30] Like Job and the other pain-bearers of Hebrew Scripture who were hints and guesses of the truth of God, and like Jesus, Word made flesh, HTM members have sought to become, with them, carriers of the Divine fate. Choosing to suffer, not to create evil, HTM members find meaning, liberation of soul, and a powerful intercession for the world. It shows in microcosm what could be done in macrocosm—nationally, internationally—and so becomes light and leaven. HTM members have sought to follow Jesus who taught always to decide to repay every fear, hatred, and evil by innocent suffering.

Loving humility is a powerful force—the emotion, energy, and passion that belong to the incarnation. It is the strongest of all things. There is nothing else like it. It is endowed with all the energy of the incarnation and the unknown treasures of the abyss. Community members seek to

> Pray for all people of evil will.
> Let the way we live together be the prayer that is offered to God
> for the enemies of life.
> Pray for all who exploit and abuse; and more—
> Love them, but not on your own, together.[31]

Innocent suffering is the link between the righteous ones who endure suffering and the sinners who inflict it. If there were not that link, they would drift apart. Sinful and righteous persons would remain on parallel lines that never meet. In that case, the righteous would have no power over the sinner because one cannot deal with what one does not meet. But in the meeting healing and reconciliation can emerge, as suggested by the story mentioned in the introduction to this book of Abraham interceding on behalf of Sodom and Gomorrah (Gen 18:32).[32]

THE PRACTICE OF HUMILITY

"For us there is only the trying, the rest is none of our business."

Often, contemporary society and religion embody an ethos that recalls ancient words, "The day is short; there is much work to be done," or, "It is not up to you to finish the work, yet you are not free to avoid it."[33] By

---

30. de Beausobre, *Flame in the Snow*, 12.
31. HTM, "Testament and Pastoral Rule," 24.
32. Bloom, *Living Prayer*, 19; Wiesel, *Legends of Our Time*, 125–29.
33. Kravitz and Olitzky, *Pirke Avot*, 29–30.

contrast, the tenth and final part of the Resolve comes from T. S. Eliot, "East Coker, Four Quartets," where he comments to the effect that each venture represents a new beginning; our part is the trying merely, gain or loss is not our affair.[34]

HTM members witness to a God who is revealed as "Holy Community." Humbly, members offer their own experience of transfiguration as a model for human fulfillment and service in our world. They do not strive actively for numerical growth or power, and have found that any thought of achievement such as these indices of worldly success is an attempt at control of their lives, and of the life of the world. But while the work that is done is not for members to complete, it is nonetheless not the case that there is no trying. In the totality of their lives, members seek greater intimacy between God and the human soul.

HTM members do not worry about survival in terms of vocations or recruitments. They trust God and float, to paraphrase Brother Roger of Taizé, on the safe waters of life as it comes, with all the rough weather it may bring![35] Members give without counting how many years are left. Without undue concern for the long-term survival of HTM, members cite Simone Weil, "It is not my business to think about myself. It is my business to think about God. It is for God to think about me."[36] Similarly, Jonathan Wilson-Hargrove of Rutba House states, "Whether these [new monastic] communities proliferate or not, this life is good enough in itself."[37]

Concluding Reflections

In books included in the bibliography, Robert Bellah, Clive Hamilton, Parker Palmer, Robert Putnam, David Tacey, and other insightful analysts of western, postmodern society have identified loss of community, rampant materialism, and extreme individualism as among the sources of extraordinary stress in the lives of people. Many fend off unwanted feelings such as insecurity, unhappiness, and despair by engaging in a continuous quest to find happiness apart from their truest selfhood.

---

34. Elliot, *Complete Poems and Plays*, 128.

35. Shultz, *Life We Never Dared Hope for*, 69. A deranged woman murdered Brother Roger on August 16, 2005.

36. Weil, *Waiting on God*, 20.

37. Byassee, "New Monastics," 47.

As an antidote to loss of community, greed, addiction, and lack of concern for the common good, HTM members have recovered powerful practices manifest in early Christian life and now, again, in the Community of the Transfiguration and in other new monastic communities. At a time when many perceive Christianity to be bankrupt, the new monastics offer a path of wisdom, hope, and genuine interdependence.

During the spring 2006 term, I co-taught a course on prayer with Cantor John Kaplan of Temple Israel in Memphis. We were interested especially in *kabala,* Jewish mystical prayer. There are many stories about the divine glory, or *shekina,* that shines on persons. In one text, the ancient rabbis explored where God's *shekina* was found. Why did God reveal the glory of the Godself in a burning bush? Why to Moses of all people? To show there is no place and no person where God is not.

Recently I attended a gathering of several hundred Methodists in Birmingham, Alabama. A bishop just returned from drought-stricken Africa said it was God-forsaken. A woman rose and challenged him, saying, "No place exists that is God-forsaken!" Everybody participates in God's great Transfiguration. Everybody: Jacob, Joseph's brothers, Potiphar's wife, Moses, Elijah, women caught in adultery, Zacchaeus. HTM members—everybody.

HTM reflects this understanding when it acknowledges that God seeks the Godself in each of us. At Compline, members reflect on the sorrow of God that humans often cannot find the Godself within because we do not dare to believe or trust the incredible truth that God can live in us, that we are God's manifestation in the world, God's epiphany—in words of the Little Prince, "the essential is invisible to the eye."[38]

Many have come to the Community of the Transfiguration after some horrific experience. The path members have taken is one of psychological openness, transparency, and a spirituality of life that is not imposed. Through prayer, silence, and transparency, members try to respond to the evil they have suffered in a non-messianic approach. They have responded with self-acceptance, gratitude, and hospitality. By positive ways of Gospel-focused, moral, and ethical living, Community members have been enabled to contain and transfigure the rage many people have felt whenever they have suffered abuse or other evil.

38. Merton, in Skinner, *Wisdom of the Cloister,* 183–84; St. Exupéry, *Little Prince,* 70.

HTM offers safety to those who come. Two contemporary church leaders have renewed the call for creation of such a circle of healing. Gordon Cosby of the Church of the Saviour has reiterated that authentic Christianity is found in a community rooted in Christ. Community is the seedbed and the garden essential to help in bringing about the kingdom of earth.[39]

Similarly, Brian McLaren of the emerging church movement has shared his commitment to community building. Christians engaged in real communities of spiritual practice are capable of the serious work of doing theology and living as Christians that is required today.[40]

At HTM, life in Christ is centered not on a body of doctrine but on a Person, and is grown not in structures but in relationships, first with the One who calls people to Himself, and then with those one is called to live with. Over a lifetime of living into the values of their Resolve, the brothers and sisters have come to live faithfully as monks. They invite others to join them in an exciting journey, the path of community. While it may be uncomfortable to some, this path has enabled Community members to turn their backs from whatever has held them in chains and to reclaim their truest identity as daughters and sons of the living, nonviolent God. For each, in words of an anonymous writer,

> . . . the day came
> When the risk to remain tight in bud
> Was more painful
> Than the risk it took to blossom.[41]

---

39. Devers and Cosby, *Handbook*, 6.

40. McLaren, "Foreword," viii.

41. HTM, "Testament and Pastoral Rule," 9

FIVE

Why the New Monasticism Matters

Throughout history, there have never been many monks, yet the world has often depended on them. Today, there are still not many monks, yet the world desperately needs them. HTM and other new monastic communities offer a countercultural way forward rooted in the messianic lifestyle of Jesus and the early disciples.

The tidal wave of rampant hedonism, materialism, and individualism that inundated western, postmodern societies now washes over emerging economic dynamos such as China and India. The way western culture is organized and is influencing the world cannot be sustained indefinitely. We have let legitimate needs justify our greed for the fragile resources of earth with the result that current models of arranging society organization and fostering economic development threaten survival not only of human life, but of earth itself. We are destroying not only our natural world, but our very humanity.

A comment made by an African to Claire Woodley Aitchison at the Fourth World Conference on Women in Beijing, China, illustrates this assessment. "We are worried that you [United States] Americans are not human. You don't do most of what makes humans human. Do all your people sing? Does your community dance together? Do you incorporate your young into the community? Do you have laws of stranger hospitality?"[1]

The renewal of traditional forms of Catholic, Orthodox, and Protestant monasticism and the emergence of a new monasticism offer

1. *Fellowship* 61 (November–December 1995) 7.

hope and a particularly fruitful path at a time of great danger. The geographic setting of the "Breakwater Community," as many have known it provides a metaphor for why the new monasticism matters. To play teasingly with the analogy, breakwaters are engineering marvels enabling all who navigate them safely to pass through places of danger or, in the case of the rock ford on the Barwon River two blocks from the Cloister, to provide the area a supply of fresh water, an at-risk commodity in Australia.

Less than an hour away, "the Rip" is the dangerous entrance to Port Phillip Bay from Bass Strait. An outlet less than a mile wide, the turbulent crosscurrents and variable depths have claimed many ships and lives through history. A natural, basalt breakwater at Point Lonsdale helps ensure ships safe passage.

Two hundred miles to the west, two breakwaters form the modern Portland harbor. Offering ships a safe haven from storms, the breakwaters permit economic activity for the benefit of many people, but not everyone. By channeling currents elsewhere, the breakwater has wreaked havoc for owners of vulnerable waterfront homes along the coast nearby.

So too, those who enter into the world of the new monasticism are taking a great risk, one filled with challenge and opportunity. The Community of the Transfiguration offers safe space, time, and a group of people who have become voluntary pain-bearers who absorb the pain of others and give back acceptance and care. Members have chosen to bear the discomfort of a life far from well and nurture those who accompany them along a transformative path. The journey of transfiguration requires discipline, honesty, and transparency, qualities that do not come to mind as characteristic of Australian or western culture as a whole. Having navigated this journey themselves, HTM members offer their experience to others seeking God in difficult times.

Social thinker Hannah Arendt writes that dark times surround us when the past cannot guide us into the future. By "dark times," she has in mind something other than the monstrosities of the past century that confronted humanity with the effects of technologies used for genocide and the destruction of entire cities by saturation bombing and nuclear weapons. She continues,

> Dark times, in contrast, are not only not new, they are no rarity in history . . . even in the darkest of times we have the right to expect some illumination, and that such illumination may well come less

from theories and concepts than from the uncertain, flickering, and often weak light that some men and women, in their lives and their works, will kindle under almost all circumstances and shed over the time span that was given them on earth—this conviction is the inarticulate background against which these profiles were drawn. Eyes so used to darkness as ours will hardly be able to tell whether their light was the light of a candle or that of a blazing sun.[2]

Introducing this book, I quoted evocative words of moral philosopher Alasdair MacIntyre to the effect that a new dark age is already upon us. Humanity faces horrors at least as grim as those of the past century. Environmental degradation, famine, human rights violations, terrorism, threats of new epidemics, and war threaten human survival. MacIntyre's most chilling comment was not that barbarians or catastrophic dangers are waiting beyond the frontiers, but rather that our lack of consciousness of this fact constitutes a major part of our predicament.

In the future, humanity will face cataclysmic events, variants of what are sometimes, and quite wrongly, called acts of nature such as the tsunami that inundated Asia in December 2004, or Hurricane Katrina that devastated the Gulf Coast in the south of the United States in August 2005. Humanity is on a dangerous path, a perspective deepened by my reading of recent works by a number of thoughtful authors. Titles are suggestive: *Collapse* by Jared Diamond (2004); *Dark Age Ahead* by Jane Jacobs (2004); *Catastrophe* by Richard A. Posner (2004). Social thinker Ronald Wright writes that the way we have organized life on earth

> . . . is a suicide machine. . . . wealth is no shield from chaos, as the surprise on each haughty face that rolled from the guillotine [of the French Revolution] made clear.
>
> There's a saying in Argentina that each night God cleans up the mess the Argentines make by day. This seems to be what our leaders are counting on. But it won't work. Things are moving so fast that inaction itself is one of the biggest mistakes. The 10,000-year experiment of the settled life will stand or fall by what we do, and don't do, now. The reform that is needed is not anti-capitalist, anti-American, or even deep environmentalist; it is simply the transition from short-term to long-term thinking. From reckless-

2. Arendt, *Men in Dark Times*, ix–x.

ness and excess to moderation and the precautionary principle.

. . .

We are now at the stage when the Easter Islanders could still have halted the senseless cutting and carving, could have gathered the last trees' seeds to plant out of reach of the rats. We have the tools and the means to share resources, clean up pollution, dispense basic health care and birth control, set economic limits in line with natural ones. If we don't do these things now, while we prosper, we will never be able to do them when times get hard. Our fate will twist out of our hands. And this new century will not grow very old before we enter an age of chaos and collapse that will dwarf all the dark ages in our past.

Now is our last chance to get the future right.[3]

For several years, I have asked my students and a number of congregations, to wrestle with five questions:

1. What am I and what are we to do about the growing gap between the rich and poor?

2. What am I and what are we to do about the environmental crisis?

3. What am I and what are we to do about the children (trafficking in tsunami survivors)?

4. What am I and what are we to do about the lack of human rights in widest sense of many?

5. How are we to bring a deep spirituality to bear on all these questions?

The exiled Tibetan Dalai Lama posed these questions in 1999. He asked people to reflect on them on the eve of this new millennium, and then to act. His concern about poverty, human rights, and the environment went back several decades, when books began to appear with such titles as *The Limits to Growth*; *The Emerging Order: God in the Age of Scarcity*; *Small Is Beautiful: Economics as If People Mattered*; and *Enough is Enough*. Throughout my lifetime, serious thinkers have been warning humanity that we are depleting the very resources that fueled the Industrial Revolution and contributed to the prosperity of many.

3. Wright, *Short History of Progress*, 131–32.

In fact, humanity has entered the age of scarcity. Twenty-five years ago, I wrote an article in which I called for conversion on the part of God's people, in the biblical sense of the Hebrew *shuv* and Greek *metanoia*, a turning back to God and radical change of heart, mind, will, and action. I concluded by citing a story of a famous French military figure, Louis Hubert Lyautey (1854–1934). Having retired to a farm, he was into his eighties when he approached his gardener about planting an orchard. "But," protested the gardener, "the trees will not bear fruit for twenty years." Lyautey responded, "Then we must begin planting at once."[4]

Indeed, this is the time for our conversion. But I am not hopeful. In prosperous western countries, we have burned deeper holes into our ozone protective shield and engendered conditions that have resulted in the melting of glaciers and in other effects of global warming. Inevitably leaders of the emerging industrial nations, notably China and India, are claiming something close to their fair share of the world's resources, representing a scale of consumption the planet has never before seen. According to one recent source, if these two countries were to use as much oil per person as people in Japan already do, and if their per capita claims on the biosphere were to match those of people in Europe, we would need a full planet Earth to sustain the demands of the people of China and India.[5]

From this study of the Community of the Transfiguration and the new monasticism more generally, I briefly explore the malaise of western society and propose three compelling antidotes as foundational for a spirituality by which people may address the dangers humanity confronts. They are a simple lifestyle; a listening heart; and a deepened appreciation for our truest humanity with an inescapable connection with God and the entire Creation with which we are blessed.

SLOWING DOWN AND SIMPLIFYING

A disease that threatens to infect my life and western society as a whole is an obsessive belief that time is getting away, that there is never enough of it, that I must go faster and faster to keep up, and that I am pleasing God and others by being busy with a dozen jobs at the same time. To

4. Dekar, "Party Goes On," 129.
5. Flavin, "Preface."

give this disorder a name, physician Larry Dossey coined a phrase "time sickness."[6]

Since this concept surfaced in 1982, things have gotten worse. So much of life in western society is dictated by dates in a diary, a clock on the wall, a watch on one's wrist, and deadlines to which we (voluntarily) acquiesce. Blinded by an apparently endless quest for more—more achievement, more love, more possessions, more power, more results, more visible and tangible success, and many other mores—we find it impossible to slow down.

Our cultural obsession with time is manifestation of a broader cultural phenomenon, that of an unbridled excess of desire. We "need" too much. We want too much. We expect too much. As a consequence, we are paying dearly in terms of sickness, broken relationships, and empty lives.

Is there a cure for time sickness? Is it possible to slow down? Is it possible to live more simply? Monastic spirituality extends to everyone the possibility of pacing life more contemplatively and of discovering that God alone provides enough. If we but slow down and simplify our lives, we will hear God, find God, and measure life as good because God has embraced us. In words of Thomas Merton, "Let me seek, then, the gift of silence, and poverty, and solitude, where everything I touch is turned into prayer: where the sky is my prayer, the birds are my prayer, the wind in the trees is my prayer, for God is all in all."[7]

Members of HTM and of other new monastic communities have been led by the God they encounter in silence, worship, their life together, and the world to make significant changes in lifestyles. Often, they have relinquished larger incomes and status and moved from affluent neighborhoods to live in community and in solidarity with those who are more underprivileged. The new monastic communities have sought and found ways to reduce over-consumption and to share goods communally. Seeking to be a sign of the reign of God, they offer a profoundly countercultural presence in the world.

A Listening Heart

A second feature of the monastic spirituality of the Community of the Transfiguration and of other new monastic communities is a listening

6. Cited by Honoré, *In Praise of Slow*, 3.

7. Merton, *Thoughts in Solitude*, 94.

heart. In community, one truly learns to listen. Henri Nouwen (1932–1996), much-loved author and priest, reflects on the so-called parable of the lost son (Luke 15:11–32). Whether the lost son is the younger, or the older son, he must learn to let God touch, forgive, and receive him. Continuing, Nouwen observes,

> for that you need to be available; you have to be home. You have to have an address if you want to be addressed. You have to be at home in order to receive a guest or to receive God. So disciplines are ways of creating a space, a home within, in which God can come into your life to forgive you, to heal you, and to bring you many gifts. The first discipline is listening. The word listening in Latin is *audire*. And if you listen with great attention the words are *ob audire*. That is the word for "obedience." The word obedience means listening. If you are not listening, you are deaf. The Latin word for deaf is *surdus*, and if you're actually deaf, you're *ab surdus*. The "absurd" life is a life in which you're not listening. An obedient life is a life in which you are listening.[8]

Other spiritual writers acknowledge the importance of listening to God and to one another. In *Life Together*, German theologian Dietrich Bonhoeffer encourages us to think of listening as a practice of the evangelistic life. He writes, "The first service that one owes to others in the fellowship [Christian community] consists in listening to them. Just as love to God begins with listening to His Word, so the beginning of love for the brethren is learning to listen to them. It is God's love for us that He not only gives us His Word but also lends us His ear."[9]

Douglas Steere of the Religious Society of Friends also stresses the ministry of a listening heart. We are to listen "discerningly" to the other person. This requires maturity, "a certain self-transcendence, a certain expectation, a patience, and openness to the new. In order really to listen, there must be a capacity to hear through many wrappings, and only a mature listener, listening beyond the outer layer of the words that are spoken, is capable of this."[10]

We do not readily listen. In a confessional mode, I acknowledge that listening has been a challenging discipline as I have entered the world of monastic spirituality. Whether during retreats at the Abbey of

8. Nouwen, *Lenten Reflections on the Prodigal Son*; also Nouwen, *Compassion*, 36.

9. Bonhoeffer, *Life Together*, 97.

10. Steere, *On Listening to Another*, 207.

Gethsemani, during my stays at HTM, or elsewhere, my attention—at least initially—wanders all over the place. It is easier to worry about what I might say than it is to listen to the one to whom I should be paying attention: God, a brother, a sister, or the pain of my own heart.

Good listening takes energy. Good listening can consume time. Good listening may overwhelm or become emotionally draining for both the listener and the one sharing. At the same time, good listening can be an act of sacredness in which someone entrusts you with the essence of their being, and the utter completeness of what they feel.

In my experience at HTM, genuine listening to another allows the other to become a channel through whom God is speaking. I have learned to listen to God and to heed God speaking in and through the other. When I listen simply to listen or to be aware, I direct my concern wholly to God and to others, heeding and hearkening to the "thou" in genuine relationship. In words of philosopher Hans Gadamer, "belonging together always also means being able to listen to one another."[11]

How do we listen to God? Waiting on God is a major path in the spirituality of listening. The monastic practice of prayer entails being still and opening heart and mind to God that we may hear God. "Be still, and know that I am God!" (Ps 46:10) literally means letting our hands fall that we embrace God, relying on God in everything.

"Set a guard over my mouth, O Lord, keep watch over the door of my lips!" (Ps 141:3). How often, when I have prayed, have I not kept watch over the door of my lips! For years I did not. My pattern of prayer centered on talking. Gradually have I learned that growth in prayer necessarily involves talking to God less and listening more for the word God has for me.

This is not to suggest that I cease showering God with words of adoration, confession, petition, thanksgiving, and self-abandonment. It is crucial to praise God and express devotion to God. But God has helped me to learn how important it is to wait upon God in silent expectation until I discern when God wants me to speak. To hear God, I must quiet myself, become aware of God's presence and attend to God's Word. The Lord is good to those who wait for him, to the soul that seeks him. It is good that one should wait quietly for the salvation of the Lord (Lam 3:25–26).

11. Quoted by Fiumara, *Other Side of Language*, 8.

In listening to God, we allow a crucial place for silence. The nature of silence, as a context in which deep listening can happen, is described in lines of a classic Chinese text:

> We put thirty spokes together and call it a wheel;
> But it is on the space where there is nothing that
> the utility of the wheel depends.
> We turn clay to make a vessel;
> But it is on the space where there is nothing that
> The utility of the vessel depends.
> Therefore just as we take advantage of what is,
> We should recognize the utility of what is not.[12]

What if God appears to be silent? It is possible, of course, that God is not silent, but rather that we are not hearing what we want. It is also possible that God is silent. Divine silence can be positive. Thomas Merton writes of a "silence that ought to be sweet with the infinitely productive darkness of contemplation."[13]

God's silence may elicit fear and terror. We cannot pray. We sense God abandoning us. We experience what the sixteenth-century Spanish-Catholic, John of the Cross, called "the dark night of the soul," a period of anguish and dread in the spiritual life.

The spirituality invites the Christian into the path of silence. Jesus was silent before his accusers. Silence prompted Jesus to cry out from the cross, "Eloi, Eloi, lema sabachthani?" which means, "My God, my God, why have you forsaken me?" (Mark 15:34). From the perspective of the cross, God appears silent. The empty tomb proves that God was not, but this became apparent only after the fact. In our context, a culture that insists on immediate response, it is hard to be patient. Yet God's Word is not always transparent. As we listen for God, we sometimes must wait.

In her classic *Waiting on God,* French religious writer Simone Weil described prayer as paying attention. "God rewards the soul which thinks of him with attention and love. . . . We have to abandon ourselves to the pressure, to run to the exact spot whither it impels us and not go one step further, even in the direction of what is good. At the same time we must go on thinking about God with ever increasing love and attentiveness . . .

---

12. Lao Tzu, *Tao The Ching: The Way and Its Power,* 155.

13. Merton, *Seven Storey Mountain,* 410.

becoming the object of a pressure which possesses itself of an ever grow-ing proportion of the whole soul."[14] While we wait on God, God waits on us. When we wait on God and give voice to the innermost joys, concerns, and longings of our hearts, we inevitably find, God is already listening to us and giving our lives direction.

Crucial to a listening heart is listening to God in Scripture. Ephrem the Syrian, an early theologian, says Scripture brings us to the gates of paradise, and the mind stands in wonder as it enters. A slow, meditative reading of a particular text allows one to resonate with God's Word.[15]

There are other ways to listen to Scripture. Some find it helpful to read the Scripture straight through. I have done so more than once, though I confess that I have found myself more engaged in completing the task than listening to the Word of God. In Ps 139:1–6, we read

> Light of light, you have searched me out and known me.
> You know where I am and where I go,
> You see my thoughts from afar.
> You discern my paths and my resting places,
> You are acquainted with all my ways.
> Yes, and not a word comes from my lips
> But you, O God, have heard it already.
> You are in front of me and you are behind me,
> You have laid your hand on my shoulder.
> Such knowledge is too wonderful for me,
> So great that I cannot fathom it.

The Psalmist concludes with a doxology to God "who holds me in the palm of [his] hand." In reading these lines, one may note that the words are very contemporary, for the text is from *Psalms for a Pilgrim People* by Jim Cotter. HTM uses contemporary paraphrases such as this, or Cotter's *Out of the Silence . . . into the Silence: Prayer's Daily Round* and *The Message* by Eugene H. Peterson. Each day through the week, and over a three-year period, HTM members hear, read, and meditate upon readings from Hebrew Scripture, the Epistles, and Gospels.

Listening is not to be equated with self-absorption or with inaction. To experience the radical love of God is never merely a feeling. Rather,

14. Weil, *Waiting on God*, 14–15.
15. Norris, *Cloister Walk*, xv.

it gives rise to ethical activity.[16] Listening to God and to the Word, and living with the silence, one can be led in amazing ways.

Angela Yarber of Shell Ridge Community Church in Walnut Creek, California, recalls speaking to a fourteen-year-old middle school student named Katy. A "talker," Katy responded by handing Angela a folded piece of notebook paper on which was written these words:

> I am participating in the day of silence, a youth movement protesting the silence faced by lesbian, gay, bisexual, and transgendered people and their allies. My silence echoes that silence, which is caused by harassment, prejudice, and discrimination. I believe that silence is the first step toward fighting these injustices. Think about the voices you aren't hearing today.

Angela honored Katy's silence and observed that church leaders like Al Mohler of Southern Baptist Theological Seminary in Louisville, Kentucky, or Jerry Falwell of Liberty University in Lynchburg, Virginia, mar Christianity by attacking persons in the LGBT community. "Every person, no matter their age, sexual preference, gender, or nationality, has the right to have access to the divine, however they see divinity made manifest. Today divinity was made manifest for me in the silent handwriting of a fourteen year-old middle school student."[17]

CLAIMING OUR TRUE SELF:
A HEALING PATH TO INTERCONNECTION

Monastic spirituality highlights a positive relationship between the loving God and loving self. To claim God's radical love is to claim our truest self.

The distinction between the true and false self dominated much of Thomas Merton's writing and has greatly influenced members of the Community of the Transfiguration. To talk about the false self, Merton used various phrases depicting the self as superficial: alienated, ego-centric, exterior, illusory, or outward. For Merton, the false self did not exist at any deep level of reality. By true self, Merton understood the experience of being united to the image and likeness of God:

---

16. Members quote Rabbi Leo Baeck to this effect.

17. "Notes from the journey," *The Ridge Runner* (May 2007)—the newsletter of the congregation of my youth.

St. Bernard of Clairvaux expanded and implemented the thought of St. Benedict when he called the monastery a school of charity. The main object of monastic discipline, according to St. Bernard, was to restore to humanity, our nature created in the image and likeness of God, that is to say created for love and for self-surrender.[18]

According to Merton, modern society dominated by technology distorts our true self. Technology contributes to alienation by manipulating the false self, for example by creating false needs, distorting what is useful, and diverting people from working towards the common good. In a Chilean magazine, *Punto Final*, Merton explores these aspects of modern society as follows:

> There is a danger of technology becoming an end in itself and arrogating to itself all that is best and most vital in human effort: thus humans come to serve their machines instead of being served by them. . . . The more corrupt a social system is, the more it tends to be controlled by technology instead of controlling it. The intimate connection between technology and alienation is and will remain one of the crucial problems we will need to study and master in our lifetime. Technology means wealth and power but it bestows the greatest amount of wealth and power upon those who serve it most slavishly at the expense of authentic human interests and values, including their own human and personal integrity. Life in the United States shows this beyond question. But unfortunately, the rest of the world secretly or overtly wishes to become like the United States.[19]

Merton concludes this reflection, "What a tragedy that would be." Merton's editorial comment reflects his appreciation of diversity. It also reveals awareness that the carrying capacity of earth will not sustain indefinitely the material prosperity of the rich world. Merton's sense of social location led him to be very critical of the United States during turbulent times.

Merton struggled personally with transparency and integrity. As early as 1949, he wrote, "For me to be a saint means to be myself. Therefore the problem of sanctity and salvation is in fact the problem of finding out

18. Merton, *Monastic Peace*, 19.

19. *Punto Final*, September 15, 1967, reprinted in *Merton Annual* (1989) 6–7.

who I am and of discovering my true self."[20] By contrast, love of the God-self within is a part of claiming our truest self. Merton writes,

> The whole aim of the Cistercian life—and the Fathers of the Order are unanimous on this point—is to set men apart from the world that their souls may be purified and led step by step to perfect union with God by the recovery of our lost likeness to him.[21]

For Merton, practices such as simplicity, solitude, and silence help Christians come to perfect union of wills with God, by love. Bernard, probably the best known of the first generation of Cistercian monks, calls this union with the Holy One, "Mystical Marriage." According to Merton, if we observe these cornerstones of Cistercian asceticism, we may all claim our full humanity as God's children in the image and likeness of God.

> St. Bernard has really vindicated the fundamental goodness of human nature in terms as strong as have ever been used by any philosopher or theologian. And if the first step in the Cistercian ascent to God is for the monk to know himself, the whole life of such a one will consist in being himself or rather trying to return to the original simplicity, immortality and freedom which constitute his real self, in the image of God.[22]

This is a key theme of HTM spirituality relevant for today. In contrast with the depersonalization, individualism, and narcissism of modern life, HTM members resist cultural pressures to conform to a false self and claim their truest selfhood as beloved of God.

Augustine calls the true self a divine center; Calvin calls it a divine spark; and other theologians call it "soul." For Merton, the "real self" or "true self" is the God-given center of our being. A major theme in Merton's writings is the theme of our identity as bearers of God's image and likeness:

> we are incapable of knowing and experiencing reality adequately unless we see things in the light of Him who is All Being, all real. The Spirit of God, penetrating and enlightening our own spirit from within ourselves, teaches us the ways of a freedom by which alone we enter into vital spiritual contact with these around us. In this contact we become aware of our own autonomy, our own

20. Merton, *Seeds of Contemplation*, 26.

21. Merton, *Spirit of Simplicity*, 76.

22. Ibid., 89–91.

identification. We find out who we really are. And having made
the discovery we are ready for the love and service of others.[23]

Merton mentioned many factors that contributed to a deepening monastic spirituality and Christian humanism. He highlighted the
twelfth-century scholar Thomas Aquinas for his openness to Aristotle,
Arabs, and the claims of reason and nature; Chartres Cathedral, where
scholars were deeply intrigued by the natural world; and the School of
St. Victor for its motto, "learn everything, you will find nothing super-
fluous."[24] Merton concluded that Biblical study of the work of Christ,
monastic reform, creation of new orders, and the emergence of new
institutions such as the university made this earlier period of monastic
renewal the high water of medieval culture. Among the most notable
features were a refined use of Medieval Latin, a growing literary use of
vernacular tongues, a strong sense of the dignity of human nature, recognition of the dignity of nature itself, a confidence in the intelligibility
of the whole universe, and a program for spiritual growth starting with
knowledge of the self.

Merton highlights the idea that every person is a beloved child of
God. If we go to the heart of our lives and do not buy into culture's false
claims, we find the risen Christ one with us, alive in us. In this way, God
gifts us with strength to love and serve others, engaging the powers,
principalities, and even death. Seeking to live up to the full measure of
God's love, members of the Community of the Transfiguration let the
transfiguring energy of God's love, light, and wisdom consume what is
false and reveal what is true. This has enabled them to re-imagine God
in a liberating way and to become a beacon of hope for people and communities touched by them.

Of what possible relevance is such a perspective about the dangerous but ecstatic journey of transfiguration? How can we live it? Here's an
example: Terry Waite, Anglican envoy to the Middle East, was captured
by the Islamic Jihad in January 1987, when he went to Beirut to negotiate
for the release of western hostages. He spent 1,763 days in confinement.
In a recent interview, he stated, "We all have difficult experiences, but suf-

23. Merton, *New Man*, 39.
24. Merton, *Love and Living*, 137.

fering need not destroy us. It is possible for something creative to emerge from it."[25]

For five hundred years, Protestants have been leery of monasticism. For many, it is a form of "works righteousness," and it seems to make the Christian life more difficult than ought to be the case. The Protestant reformers of the sixteenth century taught that a Christian naturally gives outward expression of God's justifying grace in love and obedience to God. In 1520, German Reformer Martin Luther (1483–1546) wrote, "A Christian is a perfectly free lord of all, subject to none. A Christian is a perfectly dutiful servant of all, subject to all. . . . Works themselves do not justify him before God, but he does the works out of spontaneous love in obedience to God."[26]

HTM has challenged some expressions of Christianity in western cultures where there is a marked emphasis on size, growth, and success. At times, the contemplative focus of life at HTM has exacerbated tension with mega-churches in the region that give priority to a style of evangelism more appropriately called proselytism, and other expressions of typical Baptist congregational life, and modern life in general.

HTM members place their hope in God, and God does not leave them, or any of us, alone. The sisters and brothers of the Community of the Transfiguration offer a model of that local form of Christian community needed to sustain humankind and to midwife the new creation coming into being. Along with an entire generation of new monastics, members of the Community of the Transfiguration are made in God's likeness and moved by the Spirit who ". . . sits like a bird, brooding on the waters, hovering on the chaos of the world's first day; she sighs and she sings, mothering creation, waiting to give birth to all the Word will say."[27]

A PERSONAL NARRATIVE

For much of my life, I have sought an expression of church that defies the often-hollow ways held up to us as the "American dream." Several influences have directed me along my journey to God and into active involvement in the movement known as the new monasticism.

25. Clayton Neuman, "Making the Best of It," *Time*, November 27, 2006, 29.

26. Luther, "Freedom of a Christian," 53, 68.

27. *Together in Song*, #418.

First and foremost, my birth family brought together two religious traditions. When I was a boy, I do not recall any religious expression of her Jewishness on the part of my mother. I knew, nonetheless, that Jewish family members lived in Shanghai, China, in Australia, and in Eastern Europe. At the culmination of the Chinese revolution, my family helped some relatives immigrate to North America. I met them soon thereafter. I had not been raised in a manner to understand their spirituality, but I grew close to them. Later, I met other Jewish relatives in Israel and Australia and grew in my sense of being a part of the people Israel.

In particular, my identification with the people Israel deepened when, on the June 6, 1967, I first heard news of the Six-Day War. I called Uncle David Burstein and asked if we would survive. When I accepted a call to teach in a Christian seminary, David charged me, "Be a bridge bringing Jews and Christians together," a challenge I have sought to fulfill. For example, I have designed worship services and courses that promote dialogue and understanding; I have offered a course on Christian Prayer in a Religiously Plural World at Memphis Theological Seminary, co-taught with John Kaplan, Cantor of Temple Israel.

I was baptized into the body of Jesus Christ as an Orthodox Christian. In effect, Mother deferred to Father. Too young to understand Russian Orthodoxy, I was content to observe the main events of the Christian calendar. For example, around January 6 each year a priest would visit and bless our home.

Father was deeply spiritual. One tradition to which he introduced me was to pray the Jesus Prayer, "Lord Jesus Christ, Son of God, have mercy on me, a sinner." In Orthodoxy, the phrase "prayer of the heart" refers to the Jesus Prayer. By praying the Jesus Prayer, Orthodox Christians characteristically sustain friendship with Jesus and fulfill the injunction of Paul to "pray without ceasing" (1 Thess 5:17).

Gradually, I discerned a need to deepen my relationship with God and my need to be more at peace with myself and with God's creation. Around 1959, I committed my life to God. Since I confessed, "Jesus is my savior," I have experienced Christ as my peace (Eph 2:14), reconciliation with God, and confidence that I participate in the divine nature, restored as I am to the fullness of God's image and likeness (2 Pet 1:4). This new status before God and the whole of creation is not my doing. It is God's gift. My re-creation is God's handiwork, and it is still taking place.

God provided helpers along the way. When I went forward to profess my faith at a Billy Graham event, Paul Lindholm counseled me. Subsequently, he guided me in my newfound faith. Billy Graham was a Baptist, so I decided to join a Baptist congregation. Mel Pekrul administered baptism at Valley Baptist Church, where youth leaders challenged me to live out my faith amidst the pain of the world. Valley Baptist is now Shell Ridge Community Church. Over the years, this congregation has continued to care for my extended family. It remains a community of deep commitment to the Holy One in whom everything holds together (Col 2:17) and through whom we are empowered to give water from the spring of the water of life as a gift to the thirsty (Rev 21:6).

Like many others of my generation, my first exposure to monasticism came through reading the writings of Thomas Merton when I was an undergraduate student at the University of California. I was moved by Merton's social essays, specifically "The Root of War Is Fear," in the October 1961 *Catholic Worker*, and "The Shelter Ethic" in the November 1961 *Catholic Worker*. His compilation of writings by Gandhi contributed to my movement toward pacifism and nonviolence as ways to establish God's peace in a world of violence. As well, Merton's *Original Child Bomb*, a reflection on the thinking of government officials who decided to explode the first atomic bomb on Japanese civilians, fueled my passion for victims of war.

Lou Lucky cooked for the Christian house where I lived at university. One day, she invited me to her Missionary Baptist congregation. I attended. I started sharing in street preaching and community organizing. From Lou and from her congregation I learned that the economic, political, and social events touching my life were not separate from religion.

Martin Luther King Jr. popularized the vision of the Beloved Community, and it captivated me. For King, the Beloved Community was not a lofty utopian goal that might be confused with an idyllic "peaceable kingdom" in which wolves and lambs coexist in harmony (Isa 11:6). The Beloved Community was a realistic goal that could be attained by a critical mass of people committed to applying nonviolent methods to resist war and all the conditions that engender war.

In the Beloved Community, poverty, hunger, racism, and homelessness are not tolerated because human decency does not allow them to exist. All people share in the wealth of the earth. An all-inclusive spirit of sisterhood and brotherhood replaces racism in all its forms—bigotry, discrimination, prejudice, and structural injustice. Nations resolve disputes by peaceful means. Adversaries are reconciled.

Biblical teaching about human liberation, peace, and reconciliation encouraged me to take part in small ways in two powerful currents of the 1960s: the Civil Rights Movement and the movement against military engagement by the United States in Southeast Asia. I received training as a community organizer and became involved in civil rights and peace groups then active in the San Francisco Bay Area.

In the heady days of 1964, it seemed possible that we could build a more peaceful and just world. It was easy to forget that, even then, violence was threatening to undermine the gains of a movement that had maintained the practices of Gandhian *satyagraha*, or truth-force. I worked to register voters through a Missionary Baptist congregation. We celebrated when United States President Lyndon Baines Johnson signed the Civil Rights Act. A grizzled African American veteran of many campaigns stated, "We've crossed a river, there's a mountain ahead."

However much one hopes that love and trust will triumph over fear and hatred, however much one dreams that a world of peace with justice will prevail over a world dominated by war and military conflict, this is not yet our reality as a human family. While we have crossed some rivers on the way to the Beloved Community, we have some mountains ahead in the arenas of war, poverty, racism, armaments, environmental degradation, and hatred.

Wise elders not only tempered my enthusiasm, they also helped channel my energy, directing me to programs such as Crossroads Africa.[28] Upon graduation from college during the summer of 1965, I participated in a summer exchange in Chad. I met poor people suffering from the scourges of environmental catastrophe, malnutrition, poverty, racism, religious intolerance, underdevelopment, and war. I came to understand the need to change unjust social structures into ones that utilize the resources of the created order and of human wisdom for the benefit of all.

I had intended either to attend law school or to enter the Foreign Service through the United States Department of State. My time in Chad led me to want to explore an alterative professional track. As a result, I attended Colgate Rochester Theological Seminary for two years.

28. Sarkela and Mazzeo introduce Crossroads Africa in *Freedom's Distant Shores*, 37–51; for the founder, see Robinson, *Road without Turning*.

During my first year at seminary, I re-discovered Merton, not Merton who had written powerful tracts for the 1960s, but Merton who opened the world of contemplative practices to so many. I went on retreat at The Monastery of Mount Saviour, located in Pine City, New York. I spent a few days in community observing the rhythm of prayer, study, and work. The monks lived a simple, genuine, and full life according to the Bible and the *Rule of St. Benedict*.

Revitalized by the Holy Spirit and moved by the commitment of the brothers to remain faithful to the authentic traditions of Benedictine monasticism, I sensed an affinity with them and with others who follow the monastic way of life. But I was not prepared at the time to join a community of love and service.

When I was a student at Rochester, I wrestled with what to do about what I believed to be an immoral war in Southeast Asia. In a speech given in Los Angeles on February 25, 1967, Martin Luther King Jr. said, "The past is prophetic in that it asserts loudly that wars are poor chisels for carving out peaceful tomorrows. One must come to see that peace is not merely a distant goal that we seek, but a means by which we arrive at that goal. We must pursue peaceful ends through peaceful means."[29] King denounced this axis of evil: racism, poverty, and war. Evoking values of the Hebrew prophets and of the one we call Lord and Christ, King called for a restructuring of society.

In this speech, and again at Riverside Church in New York City on April 4, 1967,[30] King appealed for young people to resist the draft. At the time, Gene Bartlett was President of Colgate Rochester Divinity School. I discovered only much later that he had resisted World War II and had become a founding member of the Baptist Pacifist Fellowship. In my own experience, he was very supportive of me as I came to accept pacifism and left seminary in order to process my application to be registered as a conscientious objector and to offer myself for alternative service, which I did as a commissioned Foreign Service Officer.

In Washington DC, I discovered the Church of the Saviour. I took courses at the School of Christian Living, a training ground for participating in radical witness, and joined one of the mission groups that supported the Potter's House, a coffee house ministry where Gordon and

29. http://www.aavw.org/special_features/speeches_speech_king02.html.
30. King, "A Time to Break Silence," 240.

Mary Cosby, Esther Dorsey, and Elizabeth O'Connor became significant spiritual mentors.

In 1966, I met Nancy Rose. On December 31, 1967, we married and departed the United States for our first three years of marriage. In Cameroon, we confronted issues such as war, degradation of the environment, poverty, and violation of human rights. We dreamed that the polluted, ravaged creation might become a new creation of peace, joy, righteousness, and wholeness. Later, we wanted to bequeath to our sons, Nathaniel and Matthew, a different, better world than the one we inherited from our parents' generation. As our separate pilgrimages came together, we covenanted to grapple with the exigencies of peacemaking in family life.

In 1971, when I graduated from seminary, my wife and I presented ourselves for missionary service. Encouraged by our denomination's board of international ministries to do doctoral studies and to prepare to teach, I did graduate work at the University of Chicago. As this time of study came to an end, my wife and I prepared to proceed to Zaire. We were denied visas.

I accepted a teaching position at a state university in Michigan, and then at McMaster University in Hamilton, Ontario, Canada, where Nancy and I identified with small groups and quiet circles that fostered a better world. We worked for social change through organizations such as Amnesty International and the Hamilton Disarmament Coalition. We assisted battered women and children, refugees, and students from developing nations through MacNeill Baptist Church.

Teaching in a Baptist theological college, I launched into lectures authenticated with a freshly minted PhD. I designed a course on "the Holy Spirit in the Church." Talk of the Holy Spirit was, literally, blowing in the wind. I assembled a reading list and presented a syllabus to the appropriate committees. In the first class, students indicated what interested them in the course. Some wanted to recover a sense of God's presence in their lives. Some indicated that there were too many demands on their time. They had no time to practice the presence of God. Some acknowledged that, though spirituality was an awkward word for them, they wanted to explore this area. Many neglected themselves spiritually. Emotionally, they were rendering themselves dull and wooden. Socially, they were courting respectability.

These concerns spoke to my need for an intimate knowledge of God. Students showed little interest in either the history of the Holy Spirit, or the texts. And I was not much interested, either. I was in the middle of a personal crisis brought on by a deficient pedagogy that up to that time I had accepted uncritically.

As a graduate student in the 1960s and early 1970s, the curricula of institutions I attended offered excellent scholarship, but little occasion for spiritual growth or the work of justice. A secular realm of facts and a sacred sphere of values must be kept separate. I was not to move from teaching about God to knowing firsthand the One to whom the Bible bears witness. Again in the seminary to which I had been called to teach, I found a dearth of concern for spirituality and justice in the curriculum. Lacking both in my life, I did not experience work as enlivening. I experienced alienation, separateness, and disconnection from heart, students, and colleagues.

The course had some positive impact, but in course evaluations at the end of term, students urged that I teach the course on a very different basis the second time around. The next academic year, I did so. I removed tables. We sat in circles around a small altar in the center, with candles and icons. We spent time praying and on three-day retreat. Participants came to class each week having read excerpts from autobiographies of spiritual or theological mentors, kept a journal, and prepared to read from them to one another. We explored how theological reflection arises from conversion stories of Paul and Augustine in early Christianity, Teresa of Avila and Martin Luther in the sixteenth century, and Dorothy Day and Thomas Merton in ours. In an essay on "spiritual resources for ministry," I wrote,

> To probe our inmost selves is not easy, but neither is seeing the world in a grain of sand or heaven in a wild flower. To go down into ourselves is a matter of life or death: life or death in our Christian walk; life or death in our churches and, most certainly, life or death for the human race. In the midst of our busy schedules we must learn to ask our secretaries, spouses, and co-workers to respond to the question, "Can I speak to the minister?" not with the words, "I am sorry, she has someone in her office," but with these words, "I am sorry, she is praying." Ministry in a needy world is not so much a matter of responding to the problems,

great and small, which daily come to our attention, but rather a matter of allowing ourselves to be caught up into the way of Jesus Christ.[31]

I repeated the course several times before 1995, when I moved to Memphis Theological Seminary. Feedback was overwhelmingly positive. When I have re-connected with students from those years, they have claimed it was their favorite elective. Since my move to Memphis Theological Seminary, I have offered a course on monasticism every other year in regular term or as a short-term summer intensive. Responding to readings from monastic writers and their own experience of prayer or contemplation, students share their autobiographies and reflect on their experience of conversion, which in turn has shaped their faith journeys. The course includes a five-day retreat at the Abbey of Gethsemani in Trappist, Kentucky, or nearby in Nerinx, Kentucky at Knob's Haven, a retreat house at the Sisters of Loretto Mother House.

Again, student feedback has been overwhelmingly positive. Responding to a survey of seventy course participants, one student has commented, "The course encouraged me to seek time from my busy life just to dwell with God." Another writes of finding freedom to address a previously unrecognized spiritual hunger, "A desire to extend the love of Jesus to a hurting and suffering world." Another wants to "listen more with the heart, especially to those I feel distant from." Another affirms, "This course had a lasting impact on my life. Before, I thought to be a monk was to avoid life's challenges. I now see being a monk as one way to address life's challenges and to help others do the same. The experience gave me the courage to make some major career decisions that are still coming to fruition in my life." Yet another writes of discovering in monastic life a spiritual wholeness and material simplicity by which she has been emboldened to engage and sometimes to challenge society's excesses.

Strengthened by praying, reading the Bible, practicing other spiritual disciplines, and teaching monastic spirituality, I have been mindful that many people are filled with anger and hostility and express those feelings negatively through the movements they join. An important teacher for me has been Thich Nhat Hahn, who stresses the importance of practicing meditation, of seeking to acquire the capacity to look, to see,

31. Dekar, "Spiritual Resources," 20.

and to understand. He writes, "Peace work means, first of all, being peace. Meditation is meditation for all of us. We rely on each other. Our children are relying on us in order for them to have a future."[32]

Retreats every other year at the Abbey of Gethsemani strengthened my interest in monasticism. From January through May, my wife Nancy and I spent an academic term living in Collegeville, Minnesota, at St. John's Abbey, a monastic community of men who are seeking God through a life following the teachings of Jesus Christ and rooted in the Benedictine tradition. From this rich experience of monastic hospitality grew a deepening of my desire to participate in greater measure in the monastic life.

For a year, I went through formation as an *oblate* of St. Benedict. The tradition is rich in people who have inspired me to become what I am, one of God's beloved, a temple of the Holy Spirit. Their prayer life flows from this awareness, as does their willingness to offer themselves for the service of God and neighbour to the best of their ability.

Before I could return to take final vows at St. John's Abbey, Nancy and I returned to HTM where, in 2005, a significant surprise awaited us. HTM invited us to enter into a deeper covenant with them. This came as a bolt from the blue. Flabbergasted, Nancy and I prayed, walked, talked, and wrestled with challenges we anticipated if we became part of a monastery half a world away.

We discerned a clear call. In the sense that home is where one is truly loved,[33] we had found a spiritual home. Nancy and I became the first professed members of the Greater Community living outside Australia. Together with Community members, we developed "a way of connection." A service took place on July 8, 2005, affirming the common journey to which we have been called. Nancy and I committed ourselves to observing the rhythm of the Cloister, visiting the Cloister every twelve-to-eighteen months, and manifesting other signs of unity with HTM.

We have experienced as a gift from God ever-deepening and mutually satisfying relationships. We have maintained contact weekly by phone and e-mail. We have read and meditated on the same Biblical passages each morning, as do our sisters and brothers. We have found ways to contribute.

32. Thich Nhat Hahn, *Being Peace*, 80.
33. Haley, *Queen*, 759.

On May 23, 2001, I experienced something profound when my first granddaughter, Abigail Jack-Ellen Dekar, was born. A second granddaughter, Emma Jessamine Dekar, was born on June 18, 2004. In each instance, I felt two emotions: exhilaration because of the joy their lives have engendered, and despair because, if warnings about the effects of global warming and other crises are fulfilled, I fear for their future.

WHERE ARE WE?

While I have despaired since Abbey's birth in 2001, and Emma's birth in 2004, I do imagine that the Jubilee vision of Leviticus and the prophets can be realized; I do imagine an epilepsy-free world; I do imagine a world in which all children realize their identity as children of God; I do imagine a world with justice for all, a world free of the things that make for war; I do imagine a world free of war; I do imagine Jerusalem again fulfilling her destiny of joyfully guiding humanity in the light of God's glory with the mercy and righteousness that comes from the Holy One.

Monastic spirituality invites us to slow down, to listen, and to claim our truest selfhood. Following this path has brought me and many others to greater intimacy with God, a greater sense of self-worth, and a greater determination to nurture a new world free of bombs, racism, the worst effects of technology, media, big business, and the rest.

I can make no prescription as to the road others must walk, but I do believe it is a journey that will enable some readers to find a road to a different and better future. Together, as we walk the road of radical love, we will look back and see a path on which we will not return. Conscious of the Divine Presence acting through us to heal us and to bring new life to the world, I invite others to join in this powerful movement of renewed commitment to follow in the way of Jesus.

A life of discipleship is a pilgrimage in the company of all others who are being led by the one who first set his face toward Jerusalem. Athol Gill wrote,

> The Jesus who graciously calls us to a new lifestyle on the road is the same one who accompanies us as we journey into the future.
>
> The road to Jerusalem leads to the cross and travels on to the resurrection. The crucified and risen one calls and empowers his followers as they journey toward that day when his kingdom will

be revealed in all its glory, as his will is accomplished on earth as in heaven, and as all his people live together in justice and peace.[34]

In a vision of the ancient prophet Isaiah, earth's bounty is distributed among all persons equally, all members of society are valued equally, and strong and weak come together in common work and joy. Isaiah anticipated that day announced by Jesus in Luke 4: release to the captives, recovery of sight to the blind, freedom for the oppressed, the year of the Lord's favor.

Such a positive understanding of God's dream arises from the creative imagination of the prophets and the transformative journey of Jesus to the cross. If ever a vision of the prophets of Jerusalem has been needed, it is now. Humanity must find a way to live nonviolently, and to resolve conflict nonviolently. It is the only useful means to work for a just peace and to break the pattern of war in the Middle East and elsewhere. Yes, the world is a dangerous place. As we journey with Jesus, we may be required to suffer, and even to die. We do so as daughters and sons of God, living nonviolently, with God's realm of peace as our goal.

That which we can imagine, we can build. This I believe. God, help my unbelief. A practical dreamer, I am often given to despair. Everywhere, paralyzing fears haunt people. Powers and principalities imprison us. Spiraling injustice, violence, and ecological disaster threaten to destroy us. In thirst for a saving word, I am drawn to the life of Jesus who cleansed the temple believing that such action would lead to the inauguration of God's realm, nothing short of the transformation of the world.

With my brothers and sisters of the Community of the Transfiguration, I have discovered in a vital way that God's living Spirit is still guiding us as we seek to realize God's dream. We do not perceive the contemplative life as a burden. We are asked only to try it, to be holy, not good. Believing the Beatitudes can be lived, and in their speaking of truth to power, especially power without love, we pray to be conscious, honest, simple, and merciful. Embraced by God's radical love, we offer our journey and invite others to join in becoming instruments in extending that love everywhere. In trust and hope we pray:

34. Gill, *Life on the Road*, 309.

We cast away the yoke of this destructive age

To meet unexpected joy and weariness,

Undeserved love and affliction,

Illness and failure—but never alone.

You [God] give us community as healing gift in our exile,

And insight, patience and compassion as guardians on our
  way home.[35]

---

35. HTM, "Sabbath Liturgy."

Prayers from HTM[1]

1.

Lord of Life,
You drive us out into the wilderness.
You expose our political agendas,
our social and religious abuse of power.
You tell us—Be holy as I am.

O God, You turn from the evil You are about to do, and so often at
the pressure and influence of those who truly respected You and
approached You putting their very existence at stake.
Theirs was a dangerous hope—a daring resistance to Your immediate
intentions. They opened up new possibilities of hope and an
authentic relationship with You.
They had an honesty and a yearning beyond submissiveness and
passivity.
They guessed and hinted at what was coming—the incarnation of Your
True Self—Jesus.

   —A Brother of the Community

---

1. Numbers 1–4 are opening statements for liturgies; numbers 5–7 are openings
for Morning Prayer; numbers 8–15 are closing prayers for an office or liturgy, numbers
16–17, are blessings for pilgrims leaving the monastery.

2. THE HOLY CROSS

Glory to You, Lord Jesus Christ,
on the cross You reveal what no one wants to see:
that humankind is never the victim of God—
but God is the victim of humankind.
Your suffering exposes our violence
and reveals the heart of a God who alone is worthy of worship—
who does not oppose force by force, nor does He threaten;
who has no desire for human sacrifice, nor need to be appeased,
nor honor to be satisfied—
whose desire is to create life, not destroy it,
whose need is to give first and wait,
and whose honor is to serve the least and dwell in the most broken.
You defeat evil by chosen weakness,
You redeem the world by a love that desires no power,
and therefore is power.

    —A Sister of the Community

3. THE REIGN OF CHRIST

Blessed is the Kingdom of our God
the Father, the Son and the Holy Spirit. Amen.

Blessed are You Lord God Pantokrator,
worthy of worship and trust, glory and power,
holding all things together.
You carry in Your Being yes and no, light and darkness,
good and evil, lion and lamb,
holding in tension the opposites we would cancel or deny.
In the cross of Jesus You show us the choice You made before the
    foundation of the world—overcoming evil by suffering its violence
and dying rather than destroying.
Blessed is the Lamb at the heart of the universe.
From Your side flows a river of life—water for all!
and on its banks, the tree whose leaves will heal the nations.
Forgive us, O God, for stubbornly continuing to picture You with iron
    fist,

for claiming that You are always on our side.
Renew the vision of You as a wise and just guardian of the people,
curbing the power of those who would harm,
bearing in Yourself what is yet unresolved.

 —A Sister of the Community

4. THE COST OF A NEW BEGINNING

The cancellation of a debt means death to rights, revenge and
the lust for recompense.
For us it means vulnerability—
for the other it means life.

Lord,
Infected by memories and words that are sharp and bitter, it is hard to
  resist the desire for revenge and recompense.
Give me courage, Canceller of my debts—
courage 'to be'—beyond my desire.
As I begin to follow You and cancel others' debts,
create a calm and glowing center within.
Reveal that Self You created me to be and Jesus has revealed to us.
As I resist and forgive the cruelties of others,
help me to refuse all collusion with evil—
help me to be strong in suffering it
without ever creating it.
Keep me steady when I arouse unresolved conflicts and prejudices in
  others,
whose debt to me I now long to cancel.
Free them from their prison too.
Amen.

 —A Brother of the Community

5. THE BAPTISM OF JESUS: Tuesday Morning Office

This morning we embrace the mystery into which we are baptized:
that the source of our salvation emerged from His hiddeness.
Feeling His own doubt, He answered the Father's call.

He went down into the waters of unconsciousness, not knowing who He
was.
And He went under the waters, not knowing if He would return.
And He came up and out of the waters, not knowing His destination—
coming into the embrace of His heavenly Community—His true self
revealed.

This is the mystery into which we are invited:
that we might experience the emergence of our true self, our Christ Self,
in an ever deepening rhythm of
birth and death,
dying and rising,
loving and being loved,
and having been given such a gift that we might in gratitude do the
only thing that will keep this new life alive: give our self for another.
Amen.

—A Brother of the Community

6. THE TRANSFIGURATION OF JESUS:
Wednesday Morning Office

Lord Jesus, You lived on earth with no advantage to us. You felt the
depths of emotion and feelings we do—the full energy of the
opposites within that seem to tear us apart.
Is it Your owning of, and wrestling with, the opposites within You that
makes Your love and compassion so inviolable and unconquerable?
Is it this transformed energy that cannot be contained, that bursts forth
from Your body as light on the mountain of Your Transfiguration?
Is this the source of the energy with which You bring order and ease and
life to diseased bodies and minds?
Lord Jesus, help us to follow You and know You nearer than our next
breath, as we wrestle with the opposites within us,
that their energy not be transferred but transfigured
and that we may become sources of healing and liberation for others, as
You were. Amen.

—A Sister of the Community

7. THE LAST SUPPER: Thursday Morning Office

This morning we contemplate a hidden mystery made present in
 bread and wine. The reconciliation of humanity and God—the final
 revelation of the truth that God does not require payment or sacrifice
 or blood.
We are loved and desired by God for who we are.

Here is present the nonviolent incarnation of divine love which did
 not condemn us for our worst, and the faith of human love which
 believed
in a new reality that was as yet unseen.
A human being who was fully alive and who suffered the projected rage
 of the collective and repressed shadow of humanity, and did not
 retaliate.

Here in the stillness and the physical reality of bread and wine,
love reaches out to us, embracing our brokenness.
Let us acknowledge the truth and open ourselves to accept this love
which is balm to the wounds of time and rain to the drought within.
 Amen.

 —A Brother of the Community

8. Dear Lord, in ancient times you were so often portrayed as a Warrior
God to be feared, whose justice and vengeance burned hot against those
who did not measure up to the purity of Your standards. Yet there were
also prophets with the courage and clear sight to penetrate through the
curtain of the common theology of the day to the truth that it obscured.
To the violence and vengeance the people practiced and projected onto
You, Your prophet answered with Your words:
"See, the former things have come to pass, and new things I now
 declare; before they spring forth, I tell you of them."
And this was Your cry about Your Servant, Your Chosen:
"I have put my Spirit upon him. . . . He will not cry or lift up his voice,
 or make it heard in the streets; a bruised reed he will not break and a
 dimly burning wick he will not quench; he will faithfully bring forth
 justice."

And so You declared that justice could be brought about without violence or vengeance or sacrifice. Lord, we still need to hear these words, for the message has not gotten through to so many, thousands of years later. Raise us and others up as a prophetic voice to show Your true nature by the way that we live, in and through Jesus, Your true and living Word. Amen.

—A Brother of the Community

9. Dear Lord, was it really Your will that Your Son Jesus should be tortured and crucified? Or rather were You whispering or crying in the hearts of Caiaphas and Pilate and Herod and the crowds and the Roman soldiers: 'Don't do this, this is my beloved Son, listen to Him.' Was it truly Your will, or did it break Your heart when they closed their hearts to You and chose not to honor Jesus but to murder Him? When You created human kind in Your image, you irrevocably gave them the freedom to say 'yes' or 'no' to Your love. Here on the cross is the hideous cost to You of human freedom. Our hearts go out to You, dear Lord, whose heart is continually broken in order to preserve our freedom to love or not. Let our hearts ease Your pain in this moment. Amen.

—A Brother of the Community

10. Dear Lord, in the beginning You created all things—all inanimate objects, all living plants and animals, and humankind in Your own image—and You called it all good. So was it really You who at the first Passover slew all the first-born in Egypt, high and low alike, even the innocent with no political, religious or economic power—whose only "crime" was to be born in Egypt at that time? Did you really need to slay them in order to set Your people free? Or is it a human desire for blood sacrifice that is projected onto You? And even the church has taken it on with Jesus as the Pascal Lamb You sacrificed in order to set us free. Have we really come very far? The life of the Truth made flesh in Jesus shouts an emphatic 'no' to this parody of You. He overthrew so much of what we thought we knew about You. He would allow Himself to be murdered rather than overthrow a corrupt system by force. And yet—He has overthrown it—but by self-emptying love, the most power-

ful nonviolent force in the universe. May our attempts to follow Jesus in this Way bring ease and joy to Your wounded heart. Amen.

—A Brother of the Community

11. Dear Lord, we left everything to follow You, only to discover that we have not really known You as You are, but some parody of You that we have been taught and formed in. We trust You to bear with us as we sift through and dismantle our image of You that has only served to keep us in bondage and to hold You at arm's length. We look to the life of Jesus to reveal Your true nature, and to hold us in the tension between the old and the new, between the false and the true, between the omnipotent sovereign and the intimate Father. Lord, lead us into all truth wherever it takes us, for there we will find You. We ask this in the name of the One who contains both our nature and Yours, Jesus our Savior. Amen.

—A Brother of the Community

12. Lord Jesus Christ, when You, the eternal Word, emptied Yourself and took upon Yourself our humanity, You were born not as a prince in a palace, nor in an Essene monastery, or into a priestly dynasty, but You were born as a frail baby to a mother whose morals were in question, in a stable in a strange town. Those who recognized Your coming were not the religious or civil hierarchs but despised and rough shepherds and foreign astrologers. Growing up, You learned not the military games and training in statesmanship of a royal household but rather how to shape wood and scratch out a daily living. This is indeed good news for the bulk of humanity who have lived just so. Lord, open our eyes that we may meet You in the unexpected places, in the poor ones we meet each day who have no power or status, and also in the poor cave of our own hearts. In these places may we meet You with the same wonder and reverence as the shepherds and magi and with the same infectious joy that they shared with those whom they met, so that Your name may be honored and Your Kingdom spread. Amen.

—A Brother of the Community

13. Lord Jesus Christ, when You, the infinite Word existing before all time in the Godhead, came among us as a human being, You chose to empty Yourself, and become all-vulnerable and nonviolent. We have been taught that when You come again, it will be with power, with an iron rod, and judgement in Your hand. How could You change Your nature so completely? Perhaps it is human to need You to be so, to satisfy a need for vengeance, for a severe justice that burns hot to destroy rather than to purify. No, we believe that You will indeed return, but in like manner as You came the first time—full of mercy and compassion and nonviolence, exercising no power but the power of love. Even so—come Lord Jesus. Amen.

—A Brother of the Community

14. O God, You created all things and pronounced them good. Your love permeates all of creation, it overflows with the intelligence of the innocent victim, who has no power except to love and wait. Your longing and desire is to have a deep relationship with all Your creation. Before each of us is the choice of life and death; and whichever one we choose, will be given. Help us to choose life and see, to go through the baptismal rhythms of death, burial and resurrection many times and in different ways, always for Your sake, so that the vision of the promised land is seen and experienced by all around us. Amen.

—A Brother of the Community

15. O God, Your Word is direct and simple: 'Hear my Word and obey it; blessed are those who do this.' This is the call to Your alternative Wisdom from the beginning of time, through the Prophets, to Jesus' day and now. You are life. This resonating of Your love calls us to live in relationship with You—this is always changing, limited only by our choices of attachment to the domination systems of today. Help us to go forward, out and into the promised land of true liberation. Amen.

—A Brother of the Community

16. A-gloir gu Ghia. A-athair am Mac agos am Spiorod Naomh.

(Gaelic transliteration of the Gloria)

Glory to God: Father and Son and Spirit. Amen.

✦

Brother, we set the keeping of God, Father of all, about you.
We set the guarding of God, Jesus, our Friend and Brother, with you.
We set the grace of God, Spirit Holy, our Mother, within you.
To shield you and to protect you
and to keep you safe from the mischief of the powers and principalities
    of this world, within and without. Amen.

✦

We set the keeping of God, Trinity of love, compassion and mercy, with
    you—
To aid you and to cherish you in the needs of your pilgrimage,
To uphold your courage,
To strengthen your wrestling in your facing head-on
and in your containing of your truth,
transfiguring trauma into love and peace, joy and strength. Amen.

✦

Brother, may there be the blessing of God for your return to your home
    in all your comings in and in all your goings out.
May there be the grace of God in the people sent to aid you.
Amen.

✦

Brother, the presence of God,
our love for you and our prayer go with you.
May you be enfolded from the top of your head to the soles of your feet,
from this time here to the time of our next meeting. Amen.

17. A-gloir gu Ghia. A-athair am Mac agos am Spiorod Naomh.

(Gaelic transliteration of the Gloria)

Glory to God: Father and Son and Spirit. Amen.

✦

We praise and thank You, High God of Heaven, for the presence with us
of our sister and her sharing of our lives for these few days. Amen.

✦

Sister, into the Trinity, Three-Personed God,
First and Greatest Community, we place you,
that you may be held in their Being,
kept in love, peace and safety,
sustained and nourished deep within the fibers of your being,
fully becoming the Self you were created to be. Amen.

✦

May the strong protecting and guarding of God the Father, Creator of
your soul, shelter you from all mischief, within and without, that
would bring your life to naught. Amen.

✦

May the abiding joy and deep peace of God, Jesus the Word, who gives
newness of life and restores you to yourself, be encouraging you and
upholding you in your commitment to Him,
by living nonviolently and peaceably, loving first and self-giving, in the
living of your prayer and the praying of your life. Amen.

✦

Sister, may God, Spirit Holy our Mother, bless you, gracing you with
patience in your praying and in your waiting, in your watching and
in your hoping, and in the seeking of the fulfillment of the desires
of your heart, especially when you are far from home and those you
love. Amen.

✦

Our love be with you, God's love be with you, the saints' love be with
you, and the peace of the everlasting life be yours. Amen.
Blessings in the Celtic tradition, by a Sister of the Community

Alison, James. *The Joy of Being Wrong*. New York: Herder and Herder, 1998.

Allchin, A. M. *Wholeness and Transfiguration. Illustrated in the Lives of St. Francis of Assisi and St. Seraphim of Sarov*. Oxford: SLG, 1976.

Andrews, Dave. *Christi-Anarchy. Discovering a Radical Spirituality of Compassion*. Armidale: Tafina, 1999.

Arendt, Hannah. *Men in Dark Times*. New York: Harcourt, Brace & World, 1968.

Augustine. *Confessions*. Translated with an introduction by R. S. Pine-Coffin. New York: Penguin, 1961.

———. *The Works of Saint Augustine. A Translation for the 21st Century. Sermons III/7 on the Liturgical Seasons*. Translation and notes by Edmund Hill. Edited by John E. Rotelle. Brooklyn, NY: New City, 1993.

Bach, Jeff. *Voices of the Turtledoves. The Sacred World of Ephrata*. University Park: Pennsylvania State University Press, 2003.

Bailey, Mark. "St. Luke's Skete." Unpublished manuscript, 2007.

Bass, Diana Butler. *The Practicing Congregation: Imagining a New Old Church*. Herndon, VA: Alban Institute, 2004.

Bellah, Robert N., et al. *Habits of the Heart: Individualism and Commitment in American Life*. New York: Harper & Row, 1985.

Benedict. *Rule*. Edited by Timothy Fry. Collegeville, MN: Liturgical, 1982.

Bethge, Eberhard. *Dietrich Bonhoeffer. Theologian. Christian. Contemporary*. Translated under the editorship of Edwin Robertson. London: Collins, 1970.

Bianchi, Enzo. *Words of Spirituality. Towards a Lexicon of the Inner Life*. Translated by Christine Landau. London: SPCK, 2002.

Birkhauser-Oeri, Sibylle. *The Mother: Archetypal Image in Fairytales*. Studies in Jungian Psychology 34. New York: Inner City, 1988.

Bloom, Metropolitan Anthony. *Living Prayer*. Springfield, IL: Templegate, 1966.

Bondi, Roberta C. "House Churches and Alternative Communities within the Church." *Mid-Stream* 33 (1994) 435–41.

Bonhoeffer, Dietrich. *Life Together*. Translated with an introduction by John W. Doberstein. New York: Harper & Row, 1954.

Breward, Ian. *A History of the Churches in Australasia.* Oxford: Oxford University Press, 2004.

Brother Graeme Littleton. "Festival Letter—Epiphany 2005." Unpublished manuscript.

Brother Lawrence. *The Practice of the Presence of God: Being Conversations and Letters of Nicholas Herman of Lorraine.* Old Tappan, NJ: Revell, 1958.

Brother Roger Schultz. *A Life We Never Dared Hope for.* Oxford: Mowbray, 1980.

Brown, Peter. *The Rise of Western Christendom: Triumph and Diversity,* AD 200–1000. Malden, MA: Blackwell, 1996.

Brueggemann, Walter. "A Gospel Language of Pain and Possibility." *Horizons in Biblical Theology* 13 (December 1991) 95–133.

———. "A Shape for Old Testament Theology, II: Embrace of Pain." In *Old Testament Theology,* by Walter Brueggemann, 22–44. Minneapolis: Fortress, 1992.

Buber, Martin. *The Legends of the Baal-Shem.* Translated by Maurice Friedman. New York: Harper & Row, 1955.

Byassee, Jason. "The New Monastics. Alternate Christian Communities." *Christian Century* 122 (October 18, 2005) 38–47.

Chittister, Joan D. *Gospel Days: Reflections for Every Day of the Year.* Maryknoll, NY: Orbis, 1999.

———. *The Fire in These Ashes: A Spirituality of Contemporary Religious Life.* Kansas City, MO: Sheed & Ward, 1995.

———. *The Rule of St Benedict: Insights for the Ages.* New York: Crossroad, 1996.

———. *Wisdom Distilled from the Daily: Living the Rule of St. Benedict Today.* San Francisco: HarperCollins, 1990.

Claiborne, Shane. *The Irresistible Revolution: Living as an Ordinary Radical.* Grand Rapids, MI: Zondervan, 2006.

Clifford, Catherine E. "The Protestant Monastic Community of Grandchamp: History and Spirituality." *Cistercian Studies Quarterly* 26 (1991) 227–45.

Community of Taizé. *The Rule of Taizé.* New York: Seabury, 1968.

Copper, David J. C. "The Theology of Image in Eastern Orthodoxy and John Calvin." *Scottish Journal of Theology* 35 (1982) 219–42.

Cosby, Gordon. *Handbook for Mission Groups.* Waco, TX: Word, 1975.

———. "One Committed Lifetime. Remembering Elizabeth O'Connor." *Sojourners* 28 (January–February 1999) 14.

Cotter, Jim. *Love Rekindled: Practicing Hospitality.* Sheffield, England: Cairns, 1996.

———. *Out of the Silence . . . into the Silence: Prayer's Daily Round.* Sheffield, England: Cairns, 2006.

———. *Psalms for a Pilgrim People.* Harrisburg, PA: Morehouse, 1998.

Dear, John. *Disarming the Heart: Toward a Vow of Nonviolence.* Scottdale, PA: Herald, 1993.

de Beausobre, Julia. *Creative Suffering.* London: Dacre, 1940.

———. *Flame in the Snow: A Russian Legend.* London: Constable, 1945.

Dekar, Paul R. *For the Healing of the Nations: Baptist Peacemakers.* Macon, GA: Smyth and Helwys, 1993.

———. "The 'Good War' and Baptists Who Refused to Fight It." *Peace and Change* 32 (2007) 186–202.

———. "Monastic Renewal in Australia." *Evangelical Review of Theology* 31 (2007) 221–38.

———. "The Party Goes On: God's People in the Age of Scarcity." *Canadian Baptist* 127 (1981) 59–66, 124–129.

———. "Practices of an Australian Baptist Intentional Community: Holy Transfiguration Monastery." *Cistercian Studies Quarterly* 42 (2007) 377–401.

———. "Spiritual Resources for Ministry." *McMaster Divinity College Theological Bulletin* 5.2 (1979) 17–29.

Devers, Dorothy, and N. Gordon Cosby. *Handbook for Churches and Mission Groups.* Second Edition. Washington DC: Potter's House, n.d.

Diamond, Jared. *Collapse: How Societies Choose to Fail or Succeed.* New York: Viking, 2004.

Doherty, Catherine De Hueck. *Fragments of My Life.* Notre Dame, IN: Ave Maria, 1979.

———. *The Gospel Without Compromise.* Notre Dame, IN: Ave Maria, 1976.

———. *The People of the Towel and the Water: The Spirituality of Madonna House.* Denville, NJ: Dimension, 1978.

Dostoevsky, Fyodor. *The Brothers Karamazov.* Translated with an introduction by David Magarshack. Harmondsworth, England: Penguin, 1958.

Dozier, Verna J. *Confronted by God: The Essential Verna Dozier.* Edited by Cynthia L. Shattuck and Fredrica Harris Thompsett. Notre Dame, IN: Seabury, 2006.

———. *The Dream of God: A Call to Return.* Cambridge: Cowley, 1991.

Dzenis, Anna. "The Passion according to Andrei: Andrei Rublev." *Metro* 110 (1997).

Eleven Lay Associates. "A Lay Response to the Reflections of Dom Bernardo Olivera on Charismatic Associations." *Cistercian Studies Quarterly* 32 (1997) 235–44.

Elliot, T. S. "East Coker, Four Quartets." *The Complete Poems and Plays, 1909–1950.* New York: Harcourt, Brace, & World, 1971.

Ellsberg, Robert. *All Saints: Daily Reflections on Saints, Prophets, and Witnesses for Our Time.* New York: Crossroad, 2002.

Eusebius. *Ecclesiastical History: The Life of the Blessed Emperor Constantine.* London: Bagster, 1845.

Fackenheim, Emil L. *To Mend the World: Foundations of Future Jewish Thought.* New York: Schocken, 1982.

Ferguson, Ron. *Chasing the Wild Goose.* London: Collins, 1988.

Fiumara, Gemma Corradi. *The Other Side of Language: A Philosophy of Listening.* Translated by Charles Lambert. New York: Routledge, 1990.

Fisher, Duncan. "Liminality: The Vocation of the Church (I)." *Cistercian Studies* 24 (1989) 181–205.

———. "Liminality: The Vocation of the Church (II). The Desert Image in Early Medieval Monasticism." *Cistercian Studies* 25 (1990) 188–218.

Flavin, Christopher. "Preface." In *The State of the World 2006,* edited by The Worldwatch Institute, xxi–xxii. New York: Norton, 2006.

Furlong, Monica. *Travelling In.* London: Hodder and Stoughton, 1971.

Gandhi, Mahatma. *Gandhi on Nonviolence: Selected Texts from Nonviolence in Peace and War.* Edited with an introduction by Thomas Merton. New York: New Directions, 1965.

Gathje, Peter R., and Jenny Case. "Emmanuel House Begins." *Cross-Examiner* 1 (September 2005) 1, 3.

————. *Sharing the Bread of Life: Hospitality and Resistance at the Open Door Community.* Atlanta: Open Door, 2006.

————, editor. *A Work of Hospitality: The Open Door Reader, 1982–2002.* Atlanta: Open Door, 2002.

Gill, Athol. *The Fringes of Freedom: Following Jesus, Living Together, Working for Justice.* Homebush West, Australia: Lancer, 1990.

————. *Life on the Road.* Homebush West, Australia: Lancer, 1989.

Haley, Alex and David Stevens. *Queen: The Story of an American Family.* New York: Pan MacMillan, 1993.

Hamilton, Clive. *Affluenza: When Too Much is Never Enough.* Crows Nest, Australia: Allen & Unwin, 2005.

Harris, Maria. *Proclaim Jubilee! A Spirituality for the Twenty-First Century.* Louisville: Westminster John Knox, 1996.

Hillman, James. "The Inner Darkness: The Unconscious as a Moral Problem." In *Insearch: Psychology and Religion,* ch. 3. New York: Scribners, 1967.

Hollermann, Ephrem, "From the Prioress." *Benedictine Sisters and Friends* 9 (Fall 2004) 3.

Holy Transfiguration Monastery. "The Baptist Church in Breakwater, 1869–2001." Unpublished manuscript, 2001.

————. "The Beacons." Unpublished manuscript, n.d.

————. "Constitution." Unpublished manuscript, 1989.

————. "Evening Prayer and Testimony for the Season of the Transfiguration of Our Lord." Unpublished manuscript, n.d.

————. "Holy Transfiguration Community." Unpublished manuscript, 2005.

————. "Liturgy for the Renewal of Baptismal Life." Unpublished manuscript, n.d.

————. "Noon Office." Unpublished manuscript, n.d.

————. "Religious Life. Some Thoughts for the Journey." 2003.

————. "Sabbath Liturgy." Unpublished manuscript, n.d.

————. "Testament and Pastoral Rule." Unpublished manuscript, 1999.

Honoré, Carl. *In Praise of Slow: How a Worldwide Movement Is Challenging the Cult of Speed.* London: Orion, 2004.

Jackson, Samuel Macauley, editor. *The New Schaff-Herzog Encyclopedia of Religious Knowledge.* New York: Funk and Wagnalls, 1912.

Jacobs, Jane. *Dark Age Ahead.* Toronto: Vintage, 2004.

Johnston, William. *Silent Music: The Science of Meditation.* New York: Harper & Row, 1974.

Jubilee Partners, "Affirmation of Faith." http:// www.jubileepartners.org.

Kavanagh, Aidan. *The Shape of Baptism: The Rite of Christian Initiation.* New York: Pueblo, 1978.

Keplinger, Emily Adams. "It's All about Love." *Commercial Appeal,* January 20, 2007.

King, Martin Luther, Jr. "A Time to Break Silence." In *A Testament of Hope: The Essential Writings of Martin Luther King, Jr.,* edited by James M. Washington, 231–44. San Francisco: Harper, 1991.

Klise, Thomas, *The Last Western.* Niles, IL: Argus, 1974.

Knowles, David. *Christian Monasticism*. New York: McGraw-Hill, 1969.

Kruczek, Elizabeth. "The Birth of Manna House." *Cross-Examiner* 2 (December 2005) 4.

Kulzer, Linda. "Monasticism beyond the Walls." In *Benedict in the World*, edited by Linda Kulzer and Roberta Bondi, 5–10. Collegeville, MN: Liturgical, 2002.

Langmead, Ross, editor. *Reimaging God and Mission*. Adelaide, Australia: ATF, 2007.

Lao Tzu, *Tao The Ching: The Way and Its Power*. Translated by A. Whaley. Boston: Houghton Mifflin, 1934.

Leclercq, Jean. *The Love of Learning and the Desire for God: A Study of Monastic Culture*. Translated by Catharine Misrahi. New York: Fordham University Press, 1961.

Lerner, Michael. *The Left Hand of God: Taking Back Our Country from the Religious Right*. San Francisco: Harper, 2005.

Lewis, C. S. *The Weight of Glory and Other Addresses*. New York: Macmillan, 1949.

Luke, Helen M. *Dark Wood to White Rose: A Study in Meanings in Dante's Divine Comedy*. Pecos, NM: Dove, 1975.

———. *Such Stuff as Dreams Are Made on: the Autobiography and Journals of Helen M. Luke*. Sandpoint, ID: Morning Light, 2000.

———. *Vow and Doctrine in the Age of the Spirit*. Three Rivers, MI: Apple Farm Discussion Group, 1969–1970.

Luther, Martin. "Freedom of a Christian." In *Martin Luther: Selections from his Writings*, edited by John Dillenberger, 42–85. New York: Anchor, 1961.

MacIntyre, Alasdair. *After Virtue: A Study in Moral Theory*. Notre Dame, IN: University of Notre Dame Press, 1981.

Manley, Ken R. *From Woolloomooloo to "Eternity": A History of Australian Baptists*. 2 vols. Milton Keynes, UK: Paternoster, 2006.

Marty, Martin E. "Foreword." In *For the Healing of the Nations: Baptist Peacemakers*, by Paul R. Dekar, xi–xiv. Macon, GA: Smyth & Helwys, 1993.

McLaren, Brian. "Foreword." In *How (Not) to Speak of God*, by Peter Rollins, vii–x. Brewster, MA: Paraclete, 2006.

Meadows, Donella H. and others. *Beyond the Limits: Confronting Global Collapse. Envisioning a Sustainable Future*. White River Junction, VT: Chelsea Green, 1992.

———. *Limits to Growth*. New York: Signet, 1972.

Menno Simons. *The Complete Writings*. Edited by J. C. Winger. Scottdale, PA: Mennonite Publishing House, 1956.

Merton, Thomas. "Answers for Herman Lavin Cerda." *Punto Final*, September 15, 1967; reprinted in *Merton Annual* 2 (1989).

———. *Asian Journal*. Edited from his notebooks by Naomi Burton, Patrick Hart, and James Laughlin. New York: New Directions, 1973.

———. *Conjectures of a Guilty Bystander*. Garden City, NY: Doubleday, 1966.

———. *Contemplation in a World of Action*. Introduction by Jean Leclercq. New York: Doubleday, 1971.

———. *The Inner Experience: Notes on Contemplation*. Edited with an introduction by William H. Shannon. San Francisco: Harper, 2003.

———. *Love and Living*. Edited by Naomi Burton Stone and Patrick Hart. New York: Farrar, Straus and Giroux, 1979.

———. *Monastic Peace*. Trappist, KY: Abbey of Gethsemani, 1958.

———. *The New Man*. New York: Farrar, Straus & Giroux, 1962.

———. *Original Child Bomb*. New York: New Directions, 1962.

———. *Passion for Peace. The Social Essays*. Edited by William H. Shannon. New York: Crossroad, 1997.

———. *Seeds of Contemplation*. New York: New Directions, 1949.

———. *The Seven Storey Mountain*. New York: New American Library, 1948.

———. *The Spirit of Simplicity. Characteristic of the Cistercian Order*. Trappist, KY: Gethsemani, 1948.

———. *A Thomas Merton Reader*. Edited by Thomas P. McDonnell. Garden City, NY: Image, 1974.

———. *Thoughts in Solitude*. London: Burns and Oates, 1958.

Metcalf, William J., editor. *From Utopian Dreaming to Communal Reality*. Sydney: University of New South Wales Press, 1995.

———, and Elizabeth Huf. *Herrnhut: Australia's First Utopian Commune*. Melbourne: Melbourne University Press, 2002.

Moll, Rob. "The New Monasticism." *Christianity Today* 49 (September 2005) 38–46.

Mosley, Don, and Joyce Hollyday. *With Our Own Eyes*. Scottdale: Herald, 1996.

Muecke, Stephen. *No Road (Bitumen All the Way)*. Fremantle: Fremantle Arts Centre, 1997.

Munro, Marita Rae. "A History of the House of the Gentle Bunyip (1975–1990)." MA diss., University of Melbourne, 2002.

Neville, David, editor. *Prophecy and Passion: Essays in Honour of Athol Gill*. Adelaide: Australian Theological Forum, 2002.

Norris, Kathleen. *The Cloister Walk*. New York: Riverhead, 1996.

Nouwen, Henri J. M. *Lenten Reflections on the Prodigal Son*. Audio Tape.

———. *Wounded Healer: Ministry in Contemporary Society*. Garden City, NY: Doubleday, 1972.

———, Donald P. McNeill, and Douglas A. Morrison. *Compassion: Reflection on the Christian Life*. Garden City, NY: Doubleday, 1983.

O'Connor, Elizabeth. *Journey Inward, Journey Outward*. New York: Harper & Row, 1968.

O'Donohue, John. *Beauty: The Invisible Embrace*. San Francisco: HarperCollins, 2004.

Olivera, Bernardo. *The Search for God: Conferences, Letters, and Homilies*. Kalamazoo, MI: Cistercian, 2002.

O'Neill, Dan. *Signatures: The Story of John Michael Talbot*. Berryville, AR: Troubadour for the Lord, 2003.

Ouspensky, Leonid and Vladimir Lossky. *The Meaning of Icons*. Translated by G. E. H. Palmer and E. Kadloubovsky. Crestwood, NY: St. Vladimir's Seminary Press, 1989.

Ozment, Steven. *Reformation in the Cities: The Appeal of Protestantism to Sixteenth-Century Germany and Switzerland*. New Haven, CT: Yale University Press, 1980.

Palmer, Parker J. *The Company of Strangers: Christians and the Renewal of America's Public Life*. New York: Crossroad, 1981.

———. *A Hidden Wholeness: The Journey toward an Undivided Life*. San Francisco: Jossey-Bass, 2004.

Paterson, Tom. "Family Therapy and the Good Life: The Geoff Goding Memorial Lecture." Melbourne, 2004.

Peifer, Claude J. "Historical Reflections of the Life-Span of Monasteries." *American Benedictine Review* 54 (2003) 121–41.

Perkins, John M., editor. *Restoring at-Risk Communities. Doing It Together and Doing It Right.* Grand Rapids, MI: Baker, 1995.

Phillips, Bianca. "The Caritas Village Brings Art, Veggie Burgers, and Love to Binghamton." *Memphis Flyer* #949, February 22, 2007.

The Philokalia. The Complete Text Compiled by St. Nikodimos of the Holy Mountain and St. Makarios of Corinth. Translated and edited by G. E. H. Palmer, Philip Sherrard, and Kallistos Ware. London: Faber and Faber, 1979.

Pidwell, Harold James. *A Gentle Bunyip: The Athol Gill Story.* West Lakes, S. Australia: Seaview, 2007.

Pirke Avot. A Modern Commentary on Jewish Ethics. Edited and Translated by Leonard Kravitz and Kerry M. Olitzky. New York: UAHC Press, 1993.

Porter, Muriel. *Land of the Spirit? The Australian Religious Experience.* Geneva: WCC, 1990.

Posner, Richard A. *Catastrophe: Risk and Response.* Oxford: Oxford University Press, 2004.

Prevellet, Elaine M. *Making the Shift.* St. Louis: Loretto Earth Network, 2006.

Putnam, Robert D. *Bowling Alone: The Collapse and Revival of American Community.* New York: Simon & Schuster, 2000.

Quenot, Michel. *The Resurrection and the Icon.* Translated by Michael Breck. Crestwood, NY: St. Vladimir's Seminary Press, 1997.

Rivkin, Jeremy, with Ted Howard. *The Emerging Order: God in the Age of Scarcity.* New York: Putnam's, 1979.

Roberts, Bev. *The Cultural Heritage of the Barwon River.* Geelong, Australia: Barwon Water, 1996.

Robinson, James H. *Road without Turning.* New York: Farrar, Straus, 1950.

Ross, Maggie. *The Fountain and the Furnace: The Way of Tears and Fire.* Mahwah, NJ: Paulist, 1987.

Rutba House, editors. *School(s) for Conversion: 12 Marks of a New Monasticism.* Eugene, OR: Cascade, 2005.

Saint-Exupéry, Antoine de. *The Little Prince.* Translated by Katherine Woods. New York: Harcourt, Brace and World: 1943.

Sanford, John A. *Evil: The Shadow Side of Reality.* New York: Crossroad, 1987.

Sarkela, Sandra J. and Patrick Mazzeo. "Rev. James H. Robinson and American Support for African Democracy and Nation-Building, 1950s–1970s." In *Freedom's Distant Shores: American Protestants and Post-Colonial Alliances with Africa*, edited by R. Drew Smith, 37–52. Waco: Baylor, 2006.

The Schleitheim Confession. Translated and edited by John H. Yoder. Scottdale, PA: Herald, 1973.

Scholem, Gershom Gerhard. "The Tradition of the Thirty-Six Hidden Just Men." In *The Messianic Idea in Judaism and Other Essays on Jewish Spirituality*, 251–56. New York: Schocken, 1971.

Schumacher, E. F. *Small Is Beautiful: Economics as If People Mattered.* New York: Harper & Row, 1973.

Skinner, John, editor. *Wisdom of the Cloister: 385 Daily Readings.* New York: Image, 1999.

Smith, Michael. "Holy Transfiguration Monastery." *Overacuppa: Christian Community Perspectives* 2 (1998) 4–5.

Solzhenitsyn, Alexander. *Stories and Prose Poems.* Translated by Michael Glenny. New York: Bantam, 1971.

Sophrony, Archimandrite. *The Monk of Mount Athos: Staretz Silouan, 1866–1938.* London: Mowbrays, 1973.

Steere, Douglas V. *On Listening to Another.* Garden City, NY: Doubleday-Galilee, 1978.

Steindl-Rast, David. *Gratefulness, the Heart of Prayer: An Approach to Life in Fullness.* New York: Paulist, 1984.

Stock, Jon, Tim Otto, and Jonathan Wilson-Hartgrove. *Inhabiting the Church: Biblical Wisdom for a New Monasticism.* Eugene, OR: Cascade, 2007.

Strahan, Lynne. *Out of the Silence: A Study of a Religious Community for Women; The Community of the Holy Name.* Melbourne: Oxford University Press, 1988.

Tacey, David. *The Spirituality Revolution.* Sydney: HarperCollins, 2003.

Talbot, John Michael. "A Call to a Modern Monastic Movement." http://www.johnmichaeltalbot.com/Reflections/index.asp?id=155.

Taylor, John V. *Enough is Enough.* London: SCM, 1975.

Thich Nhat Hanh. *Ange:. Wisdom for Cooling the Flames.* New York: Riverhead, 2001.

———. *Being Peace.* Berkeley, CA: Parallax, 1987.

Together in Song: Australian Hymn Book II. Sydney: HarperCollinsReligious, 2005.

Turner, Victor W. *The Ritual Process: Structure and Anti-Structure.* Chicago: Aldine, 1969.

Thurston, Bonnie. "Soli Deo Placere Desiderans." In *A Monastic Vision for the 21st Century: Where Do We Go from Here?* edited by Patrick Hart, 1–22. Kalamazoo, MI: Cistercian, 2006.

Wall, John N., Jr. *George Herbert: The Country Parson and The Temple.* Classics of Western Spirituality. New York: Paulist, 1981.

Webb, Judy. "Protestant Sisterhoods." Senior Seminar, McMaster Divinity College, Hamilton, Ontario, 1985.

Weil, Simone. *Waiting on God.* Translated by Emma Graufurd. London: Fontana, 1959.

Weitzmann, Kurt, et al. *The Icon.* London: Evans, 1982.

Wiesel, Elie. *Legends of Our Time.* New York: Schocken, 1982.

Williams, George H. *The Radical Reformation.* Philadelphia: Westminster, 1962.

Wilson, Jonathan R. *Living Faithfully in a Fragmented World: Lessons for the Church from MacIntyre's After Virtue.* Harrisburg, PA: Trinity, 1997.

———. "Introduction." In *School(s) for Conversion: 12 Marks of a New Monasticism,* edited by The Rutba House, 1–9. Eugene, OR: Cascade, 2005.

Wilson, Paul. *Calm at Work.* New York: Penguin Putnam, 1999.

———. *Instant Calm. Over 100 Easy-to-Use Techniques for Relaxing Mind and Body.* New York: Penguin Putnam, 1995.

World Council of Churches. "Christian Spirituality for Our Times." *Mid-Stream* 33 (1994) 473–81.

Worldwatch Institute. *State of the World 2006: A Worldwatch Institute Report on Progress toward a Sustainable Society.* New York: Norton, 2006.

Wright, Ronald. *A Short History of Progress.* Toronto: Anansi, 2004.